GETTING STARTED WITH THE VISION PRO

IO416415

THE INSANELY EASY GUIDE TO UNDERSTANDING AND USING VISIONOS AND SPACIAL COMPUTING

SCOTT LA COUNTE

RIDICULOUSLY
SIMPLE BOOKS

ANAHEIM, CALIFORNIA

www.RidiculouslySimpleBooks.com

Table of Contents

INTRODUCTION

Explore the revolutionary world of spatial computing as brought to life by Apple's latest innovation, the Apple Vision Pro.

This guide is not just about understanding a device; it's about stepping into the future of spatial computing. For people who own a Vision Pro, it will show them how to use it; for those just curious about the device, it will show them what it's capable of and help you decide if it's for you.

This guide delves into the functionalities, design, and transformative potential of this groundbreaking device. It's an exploration of how the Vision Pro is redefining the realms of productivity, entertainment, connectivity, and spatial computing.

You'll learn:

- **Navigating around the OS**: Unveil the intuitive interaction capabilities of the Vision Pro, including eye movements, hand gestures, and voice commands.
- **Workspace Transformation**: Learn how this device transcends screen limitations, enabling users to integrate and scale

applications within their physical environment, thus revolutionizing workspace dynamics.

- **Elevated Entertainment Experience**: Discover how the Vision Pro transforms any room into a personal theater, offering an unrivaled entertainment experience with advanced visual and audio technology.
- **Capturing and Reliving in 3D**: Dive into the capabilities of Apple's first 3D camera, allowing users to capture spatial photos and videos, adding a new dimension to memory preservation.
- **Redefining Digital Connectivity**: Understand how the Vision Pro enhances virtual interactions, making digital meetings and collaborations more immersive and effective.
- And much more!

The Apple Vision Pro is a blend of digital and physical realities, creating experiences once thought impossible. Through this book, readers will gain a thorough understanding of the Vision Pro's capabilities and the potential it holds to transform everyday life.

Note: This guide is crafted with the aim of enhancing your Vision Pro experience. While not officially endorsed by Apple, Inc., it offers a wealth of knowledge and tips to help you make the most of your device.

[1]

GETTING TO KNOW THE VISION PRO

WHO IS THIS THING FOR?!

The Vision Pro is a revolutionary device. Putting it on for the first time is... it's an experience beyond words. I could extol its immersive and lifelike qualities endlessly, but words simply can't capture its essence. It's nothing short of incredible. When I first used it, all I could think about was how, in a few years, my child might use this technology in school, potentially transforming education. Imagine not even needing to attend school physically—

students could interact and see their peers as if they were right there with them.

So, it's for everyone, right? Well, sort of, but not quite yet. If you have $3,500 to spare, then sure, why not purchase it? You might as well get one for your less fortunate friend too! However, for the vast majority of us, the Vision Pro remains just out of reach—for now. It's on the horizon; much like the iPhone revolutionized our daily lives, the Vision Pro is set to do the same. It will become more affordable and lighter. It's already excellent, but there's always room for improvement.

To be clear, the Vision Pro isn't a beta product. It's a polished device that outperforms any other of its kind. It's not even a fair comparison to other headsets.

But who is it actually for? There are numerous applications. Developers, for instance, are a primary audience; if you're looking to be at the forefront of a technology that will reshape our work and interactions, then the Vision Pro is essential. It's a must-have for understanding and creating for this new platform. For those who travel frequently, the Vision Pro is a game-changer, offering a vast virtual office space when physical space is limited. This is equally true for remote workers without a dedicated workspace; it enables focus in less-than-ideal environments—just make sure you have a comfortable chair to avoid neck strain, which can occur even with good support. It's also the ultimate entertainment device for movie enthusiasts; it promises an experience superior to any television you might own, though it does come with a caveat of isolation—you can't share a movie on the couch with someone unless they have their own headset.

If you're concerned about migraines and motion sickness, rest assured that these issues are less about the experience and more about the device's weight causing muscle strain. While individual experiences may vary, most agree that the motion sickness associated with other headsets is not an issue with the Vision Pro. You might feel a bit odd the first few times you remove it, but this is largely due to the level of immersion—your brain is adjusting to new experiences. It's important to ease into it gradually. Don't rush into active movement; instead, sit back, relax, and acclimate to this novel experience. I would recommend doing no more than 20 or 30 minutes at a time when you first start using it; and I know it's going to be really tempting to push the limits because of how fun it is.

We are on the brink of a technological revolution, and as new applications are developed daily, the Vision Pro will only improve. If you're not convinced that the Vision Pro is for you, that's understandable; but consider revisiting it in a few years.

WHAT IF I HAVE A MEDICAL CONDITIONS

So maybe the Vision Pro is for you, but what if your prone to get migraines, your pregnant, or have another health condition? It may or may not be for you. How can you be sure: talk to your doctor before using it.

If you get the green light from your doc, here are some pointers:

- Start seated and ease into less immersive experiences.
- Keep your sessions short and sweet, with plenty of breaks.
- If you feel any discomfort, dizziness, or eye strain, it's time to take a break.

For those with medical devices like pacemakers, hearing aids, or defibrillators, your new tech buddy, the Vision Pro, could be a bit too magnetic. So, again, it's best to consult your doctor or the device manufacturer before using Vision Pro.

If all's well, remember:

- Keep a safe distance between your Vision Pro and any medical devices.
- If you notice any interference with your device, it's better to stop using the headset.

Here are some clear signs to take a break or seek medical advice:

- Any symptoms related to your medical condition pop up.
- You're all clear from your doctor but still feel physically uncomfortable, dizzy, or visually strained.
- You notice any skin irritation, swelling, or itchiness during or after use.

Using the Apple Vision Pro can be a blast, but your health should obviously be the top priority. Always consult with your healthcare provider to ensure a safe and enjoyable experience. It's always better to be safe than sorry.

APPLE VISION PRO WITH PRESCRIPTION LENSES

What if you think the Vision Pro is for you, but your like lots of other people: you wear glasses. Good news! You can't wear your glasses with the Vision Pro directly (you can wear contacts, however), but there's a solution: Zeiss Optical Inserts. These are specially designed for the Vision Pro, catering to a wide range of prescriptions, including those for astigmatism. Sadly, if your glasses have a prism value, these inserts aren't yet an option.

Do you need them? I only need glasses for far away, so I didn't think I'd spend $149, but I'm glad I did. It's right on my face, so why bother? Because the depth of the picture can be far away. I've tried it with and without it and it's enhanced with it.

To get these inserts, you'll need a prescription that includes your full name, date of birth, and the details of your eye care professional. Remember, it should cover both your distance and near correction needs and shouldn't be expired. And here's a tip: contact lens prescriptions won't do the trick here.

If you're a fan of progressive or bifocal lenses, you're in luck, as these inserts cater to most such needs. After you send in your prescription, you'll hear back within a day about the availability of your custom inserts. It took me less than 5 hours, and even though it said it would take three weeks, they were at my doorstep at launch.

If your eyewear is more about catching up on the latest bestseller, you can opt for Zeiss Optical Inserts – Readers. They come in various strengths to match your reading glasses. But, if you find yourself squinting or feeling uneasy while using the Vision Pro, it might be time to consult an eye care professional for a more suitable prescription.

If you use soft single vision contacts, you're good to go without any additional inserts. However, hard lens users might face challenges with eye tracking. In such cases, consider the Zeiss Optical Inserts or an alternative control method, like Pointer Control.

What if you've had monovision surgery or use monovision contacts? You'll want to switch to Zeiss Optical Inserts based on an eyeglass prescription.

Vision Pro is a tech marvel that uses your gaze to navigate. But if you have conditions like eyelid drooping, strabismus, or nystagmus, this feature might not work as smoothly. Don't worry, though. The Vision Pro's Accessibility features come to the rescue, allowing you to navigate using wrist, head movements, finger gestures, or voice commands.

BATTLE OF VR

I'm sure when you heard about the Vision Pro, one of the first things you said was, "That's a lot of money! More than almost any other VR headset out there." Apple will tell you, "Well, this isn't a VR headset—it's spatial computing." But that doesn't stop the comparison from other devices. In this section, we'll take a look at three headsets: the Meta Quest 3 (arguably the most popular), the PSVR 2 (for gamers), and the HoloLens 2 (Microsoft's answer to mixed reality and one of the best headsets out there for enterprise), and we'll see how they stack up against the Vision Pro.

META QUEST 3

When it comes to VR, the one everyone usually jumps to is the Meta Quest. The headset has been turning heads for several years with each generation of the device. Let's take a look at how the two compare.

Price and Affordability
- Meta Quest 3: Priced at $499, the Meta Quest 3 is positioned as a more affordable option in the VR market. This pricing strategy suggests an aim to attract a broader consumer base.
- Apple Vision Pro: At $3,499, the Vision Pro is a high-end device targeting a niche market. Its

premium price point reflects its advanced features and is likely aimed at professionals or enthusiasts seeking the best possible VR/AR experience.

Operating System and Ecosystem

- Meta Quest OS: The Quest 3 runs on the Meta Quest OS, a platform that has evolved from the Oculus ecosystem, known for its robust library of games and applications.

- visionOS: Apple's Vision Pro operates on visionOS, which offers seamless integration with other Apple products and services. This Quest OS is not unituitive, but Vision OS proves a more unified and potentially more user-friendly experience, especially for existing Apple users.

Control Mechanisms

- Meta Quest 3: Utilizes updated Touch controllers, maintaining a form of physical interaction that is familiar to many VR users.

- Apple Vision Pro: Offers a controller-free experience, leveraging eye tracking and hand gestures. This advanced approach gives it a more immersive and intuitive user experience.

Display Quality

- Meta Quest 3: Features an LCD with a resolution of 2064x2208 per eye, providing a clear and vivid visual experience.

- Apple Vision Pro: Boasts dual 4k micro-OLED displays, which is crucial for professional applications and high-end gaming.

Processing Power

- Meta Quest 3: Powered by the Snapdragon XRGen 2 processor, ensuring smooth performance in standard VR applications.
- Apple Vision Pro: Equipped with the Apple silicon chip M2, known for its efficiency and power, indicating potentially better performance, especially in more demanding applications.

Design and Comfort

- Meta Quest 3: Offers a refreshed Quest form factor, 40% lighter and slimmer than its predecessor, focusing on user comfort during extended use.
- Apple Vision Pro: Adopts a premium, lightweight ski-goggle design; the Quest is slightly lighter, but both are heavy devices that take a little getting used to. Apple's straps do feel much more premium, however.

Sensor Technology

- Meta Quest 3: Employs front cameras for AR and tracking, which is sufficient for general VR experiences.
- Apple Vision Pro: Incorporates over a dozen cameras for advanced AR, iris scanning, which all offer a more sophisticated approach to user interaction and environment mapping.

Audio Experience

- Meta Quest 3: Includes onboard speakers and a 3.5mm jack, offering standard audio capabilities.
- Apple Vision Pro: Features advanced spatial audio with high-fidelity speakers, enhancing the immersion and realism of the VR/AR experience.

IPD Adjustment

- Meta Quest 3: Utilizes a physical adjustment dial, allowing users to manually set the interpupillary distance for comfort and clarity.
- Apple Vision Pro: Lenses adjust automatically, providing a more user-friendly experience and potentially better visual quality for a wider range of users.

Tracking Capabilities

- Meta Quest 3: Focuses on controller and some hand-tracking, sufficient for most current VR applications.
- Apple Vision Pro: Offers full-body motion capture via cameras, a feature that could revolutionize VR interactions and open new possibilities in various applications.

Storage Options

- Meta Quest 3: Starts at 128GB, with a 512GB version rumored, providing ample space for games and apps.

- Apple Vision Pro: the Vision Pro comes in 256GB, 512GB, and 1TB.

Passthrough Camera Quality
- Meta Quest 3: Features full-color passthrough, enhancing the AR experience.
- Apple Vision Pro: Offers incredibly high-resolution passthrough, setting a new standard in the clarity and realism of AR applications. The Meta Quest passthrough is grainy in lowlight situations; it's enough to know where you are in a room, but not at all like the HD on the Vision Pro.

Battery Life and Portability
- Meta Quest 3: Offers 2 to 2.5 hours of battery life, which is typical for current VR headsets.
- Apple Vision Pro: Provides up to 2 hours of usage, which, given its advanced features, is reasonable. The Vision Pro weigh about 1.3 pounds, which is slightly heavier than the Quest 3.

The Meta Quest 3 and Apple Vision Pro cater to different segments of the VR/AR market. The Quest 3 offers an affordable, user-friendly experience suitable for gaming and general VR applications. In contrast, the Vision Pro is a premium device that pushes the boundaries of VR/AR technology, aimed at professionals and enthusiasts seeking the most advanced experience possible.

Many people suggest that if the Vision Pro is out of your budget, the Quest 3 serves as a good alternative. However, I believe this comparison isn't quite apt. For those who are primarily interested in gaming and perhaps fitness, and are seeking a genuine VR experience, the Quest 3 can be a decent option if the Vision Pro is unaffordable.

On the other hand, if you're like me and require a headset for both work and productivity, with the added bonus of occasional entertainment, then the Quest 3 might not be the best purchase. Given the significant investment required for a Vision Pro, it's understandable if it's beyond your budget. In such cases, I would advise waiting for the next iteration of the Vision Pro or considering the Quest 4, depending on its specifications, which have yet to be released at the time of this writing.

While working on the Quest 3 isn't out of the question, it doesn't offer the same ease of use as the Vision Pro. It is fairly quick, especially for Windows users, since it's compatible with the operating system, unlike the Vision Pro. The main issue with the Quest 3 is the awareness that you're using it—the visuals are somewhat blurry and lack sharpness. In contrast, the Vision Pro provides an immersive experience; if it weren't for the weight of the headset, you might even forget you're wearing it.

PSVR 2

Meta Quest isn't the only game in town—especially if you want a gaming headset. PSVR 2 is designed for the PlayStation, so you'll need a PS5 to use it. But how do they stack up? Let's find out:

Display and Visual Fidelity

- Apple Vision Pro: Boasts an impressive display with 23 million pixels per panel, exceeding the resolution of most 4K TVs. This feature promises unparalleled clarity and detail in visual content.

- PSVR 2: Features two 2000 x 2040 OLED displays, along with 4K HDR capabilities. While this is impressive, it seems the Vision Pro might have an edge in terms of sheer pixel density and clarity.

Integration and Usability

- Apple Vision Pro: Offers versatility with its mixed-reality capabilities, allowing users to blend apps with their environment. The device can be used plugged in or powered by a battery pack, providing 2 hours of runtime. Additionally, it includes an external screen displaying the user's eyes, enhancing the sense of presence.

- PSVR 2: Integrates seamlessly with the PlayStation 5, connecting via a USB C cable. This integration ensures a hassle-free setup for gamers, with no concerns about battery life.

Design and Interaction

- Apple Vision Pro: Sports a futuristic ski-goggle design with a sleek and thin profile. It features a plush band for comfort and a stylish silvery hue. Interaction with the device is facilitated through voice, eye movements, and hand gestures, offering a controller-free experience.

- PSVR 2: While not as aesthetically sleek as the Vision Pro, it is designed for comfort. The PSVR 2 requires the use of tactile, light, and user-friendly Sense Controllers for navigation and gameplay.

Price Point

- Apple Vision Pro: Positioned as a premium product, the Vision Pro is priced at a steep $3,499, reflecting its advanced technology and mixed-reality capabilities.
- PSVR 2: More affordable at $549, the PSVR 2 is significantly cheaper than the Vision Pro, making it a more accessible option for VR gaming enthusiasts.

The Apple Vision Pro and PSVR 2, while both offering immersive experiences and high-resolution graphics, cater to distinct audiences and purposes. The Vision Pro is a high-end, mixed-reality device suited for those seeking a comprehensive and versatile AR/VR experience, particularly for streaming, viewing, and professional applications. In contrast, the PSVR 2 is a dedicated VR gaming headset, ideal for PlayStation 5 users looking for an immersive gaming experience.

You can play games on the Vision Pro—there's thousands to pick from when you consider all the iPad apps brought in to the ecosystem; but PS5 was built for gaming, so it's not going to surprise anyone when I say the games on the PSVR 2 are superior.

HOLOLENS 2

Finally, if you thought the Vision Pro was the only $3500 headset, then you must have forgotten about the HoloLens. Don't worry! So has everyone else! The HoloLens is Microsoft's answer to mixed reality. And I know what you are thinking: Microsoft has MR?! Yes! And it's actually really cool. They've been working in this space for years and actually have the lead on Apple in a lot of ways. Is it a superior device? Let's find out!

Design

- Apple Vision Pro: The Vision Pro sports a sleek, stylish design akin to a pair of ski goggles. Made of aluminum with a curved glass display, it exudes a modern, consumer-friendly aesthetic. This design choice reflects Apple's focus on creating a device that is not only functional but also fashionable.

- HoloLens 2: In contrast, the HoloLens 2 has an industrial look with a visor-like form factor, constructed primarily from plastic. This design is more utilitarian, emphasizing functionality and durability, which is important for business and industrial applications.

Features

- Apple Vision Pro: Designed primarily for consumers, the Vision Pro boasts a wider field of view than the HoloLens 2, potentially offering a more immersive AR experience. Its comfort is also a key feature, making it suitable for extended use. The Vision Pro's "spatial computer" powers are another highlight, promising innovative interactions with the digital world.

- HoloLens 2: Targeted towards businesses, the HoloLens 2 excels in advanced tracking capabilities and seamless integration with the Microsoft ecosystem, including various enterprise applications. This focus on professional use cases gives it an edge in environments where robustness and precision are crucial.

Price

- Apple Vision Pro: The Vision Pro is priced at $3,499. This price point positions it as a premium product, reflecting its advanced technology and design.

- HoloLens 2: The HoloLens 2 is currently available at $3,500 and $4,500 for the enterprise edition. This pricing strategy underscores its focus on professional and industrial markets, where the investment can be justified by the device's utility in specialized applications.

The Apple Vision Pro and the HoloLens 2, while both powerful AR headsets, serve different purposes and audiences. The Vision Pro is an excellent choice for consumers who value style, comfort, and a wide field of view in an AR headset. Its capabilities are geared towards immersive experiences in personal entertainment, gaming, and perhaps light professional work.

On the other hand, the HoloLens 2 is ideally suited for businesses and professional environments. Its advanced tracking features, robust build, and integration with Microsoft's suite of enterprise tools make it a practical choice for industries like manufacturing, healthcare, and education.

PURCHASING A VISION PRO

The Vision Pro is one of the most unique buying experiences Apple has ever offered. For the best fit, you can go to any Apple Store with an appointment, and get measured. If you don't want to do that, you can also do it on your iPhone or iPad (you can use your computer, of course, but you'll be referred to your iPhone or iPad to do the measurements). My advice: use an iPhone. I tried it on an iPad Pro, and found the process a little more frustrating–I was turning my head in all kinds of different ways trying to get it to scan.

The other thing I highly recommend is doing the scan two or three times. The first time I tried it, I got a medium. The next two times, small. The Light Seal also measured at at 21W and 23W. If going into the store is not an option, then you might want to pick up both, and then return the one that doesn't fit.

When you start the checkout, you'll be greeted with a page to scan your face first. It's a quick process, but make sure you have plenty of light. This isn't going to work in a dimly lit room. I had to switch rooms the first time I tried it.

If you have ever did Face ID on your Apple device, the next steps are pretty similar. You'll scan your face by looking in different directions. (note: forgive my picture below–I'm on the West Coast, so ordering the Vision Pro was a 5AM wake up call!)

After you do it once, you'll do the exact same thing a second time.

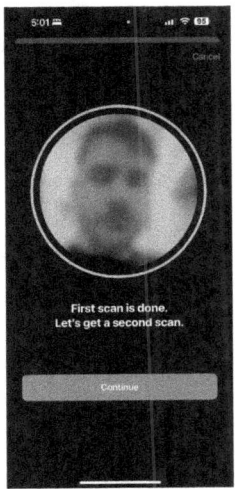

Once the scan is complete, you'll get a screen saying your face has been measured. You'll need to scroll a little to get to the next part, which is the prescription lenes.

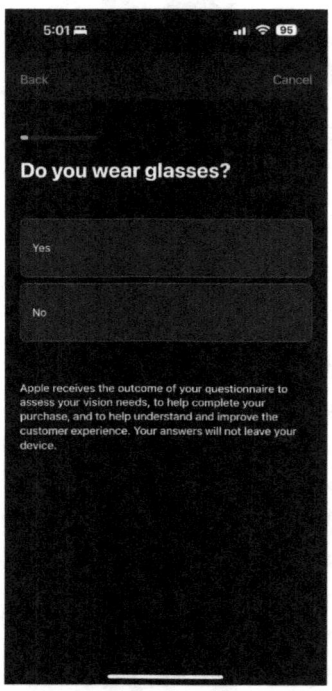

The next part of the buying process is easier—just a handful of questions about if you wear glasses, contacts, or have ever had corrective eye surgery. This will help determine if the ZEISS lenses are ideal for you.

Once this questionnaire is done, it will either tell you that you don't need the lens add-on, or it will tell you to upload your prescription. You don't need your prescription to put in an order. You can skip it and then come back and add it in later.

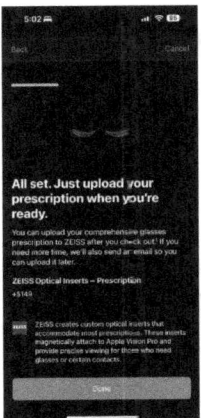

The rest of the buying is pretty standard. It will ask if you want to do payment plans, if you want

Apple Care+ (skip to the section on Apple Care+ if your on the fence about this—hint: repairs without it can cost over $2,000!), and if you want to pick it up at a store or ship it to you. Once you do all that, you can put in your order, and your all set! The entire process will take about 5 to 10 minutes.

UNBOXING

I don't typically do unboxing when I publish how to books; the Vision Pro is not the typical product, however, so I'm doing things a little differently. This section will walk you through how it's packaged.

The first thing that might surprise you is how big the box is. It's over 5 pounds and is bigger than the box for a MacBook.

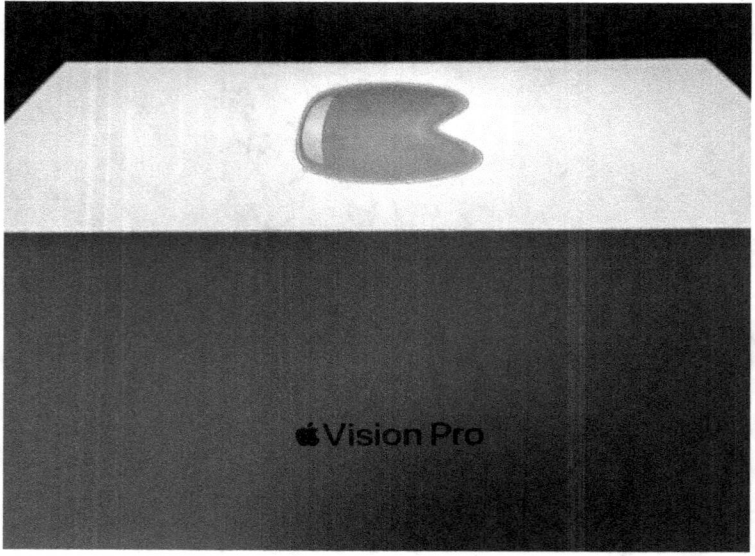

To give you an idea of how big it is, let me show you the Belkin battery pack accessory (this is an optional extra purchase), and then I'll show it next to the box.

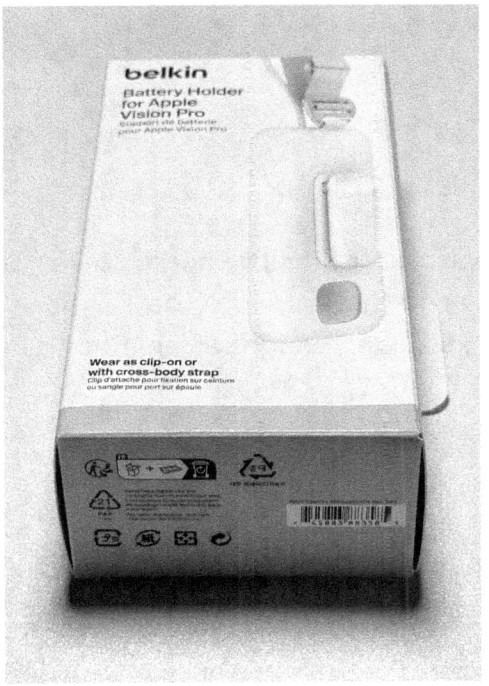

Here's the front side of the Belkin battery pack holder; it can either be clipped to you or you can use the lanyard to carry it around your next.

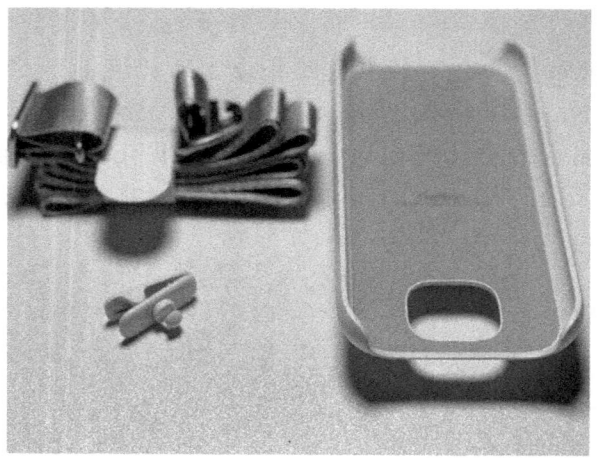

Below is the front side; and to give you an idea for how large the Vision Pro battery is; it's about the same size and weight as an iPhone Pro Max.

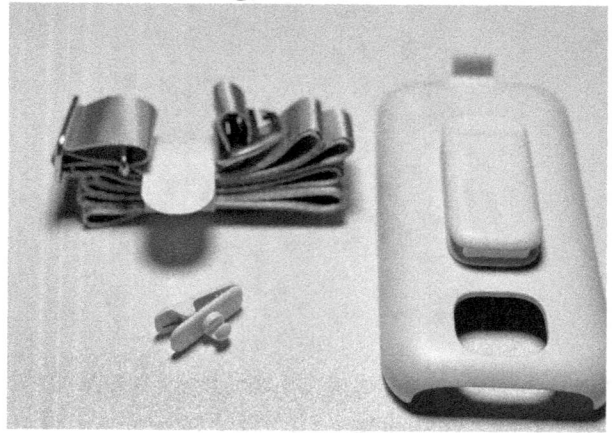

And here it is next to the Vision Pro box.

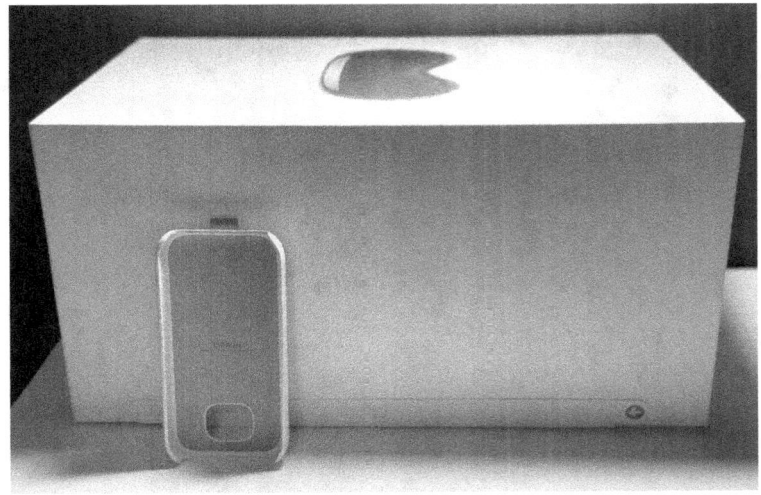

Once you peal back the easy to peel sticker attached to each side of the box, you lift the box and see the Vision Pro in all it's beauty. Some people have commented that the box can double as a nice stand. I'd agree with that, but personally prefer the travel case, which protects it if it happens to somehow fall. You'll also notice that there's a front cover; you should use that anytime you're not using the device to protect it from dust and scratches.

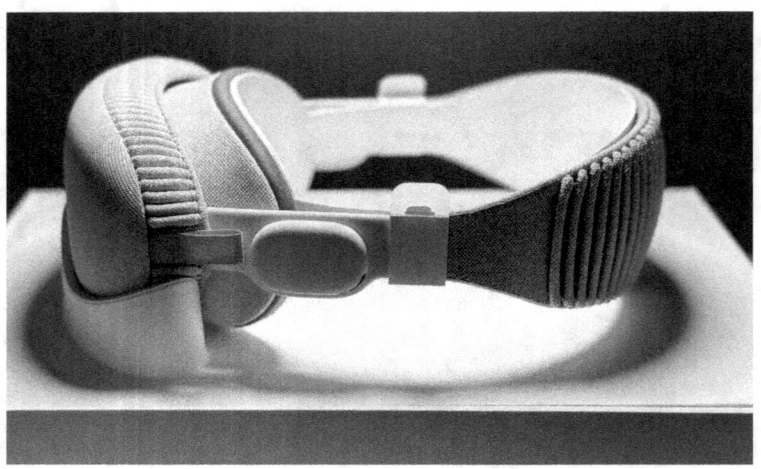

Life up the Vision Pro and you'll find the battery. A lot has been said about the battery pack; I found it to be very well build, not that heavy, and easy to either attach to you or set to the side. I didn't notice it was even there. The battery charges with an included USB-C adapter; you can charge it while you are using the Vision Pro.

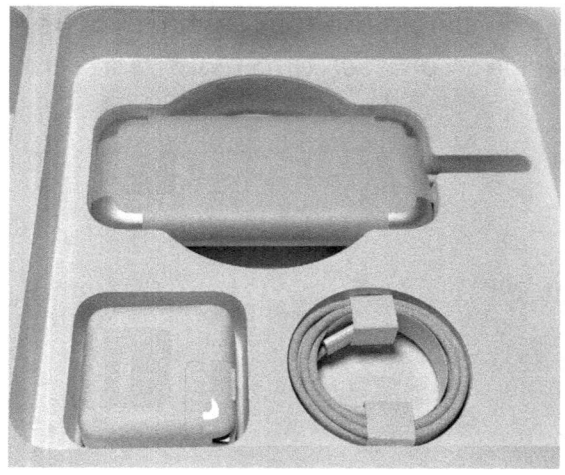

Also at the top of the box is the Light Seal Cushion. There's already a cushion magnetically attached to the Vision Pro; this one is a little bit thicker

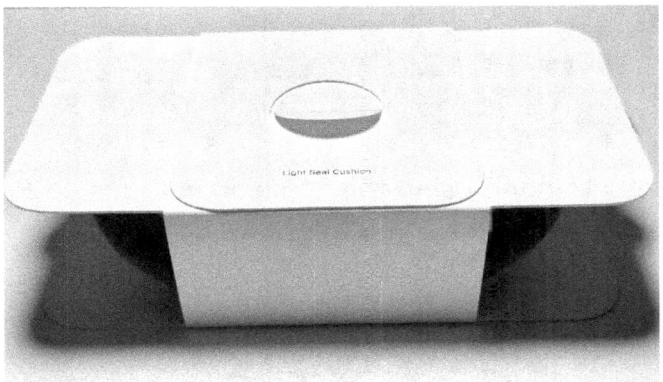

. If you are using the Zeiss lens inserts, then you'll probably want to swap it out with this slightly thicker one.

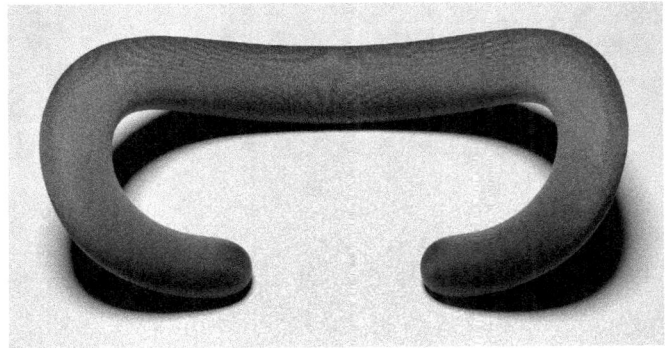

Under the Light Seal is a polishing cloth.

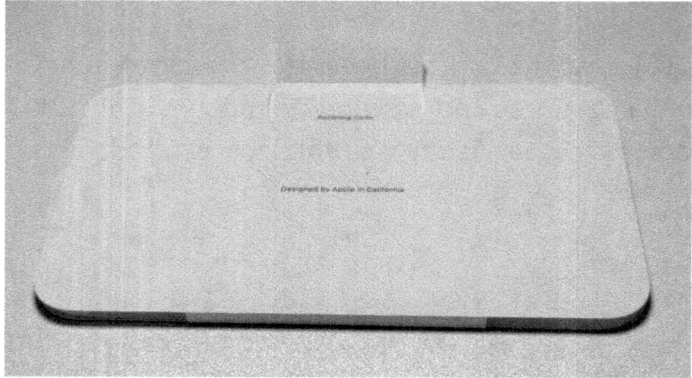

I recommend using this to clean your Vision Pro over something else you might have.

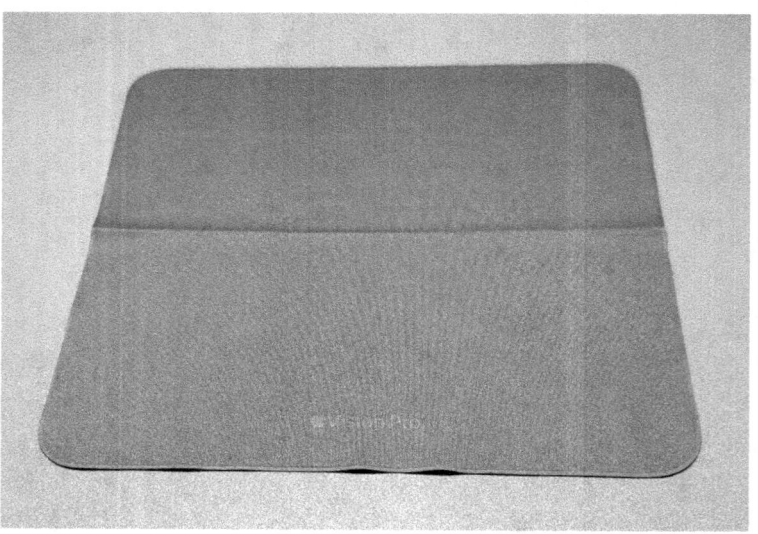

Under the cloth is the Dual Loop band.

The Dual Loop band helps distribute the weight more evenly, and many people prefer it over the softer single band.

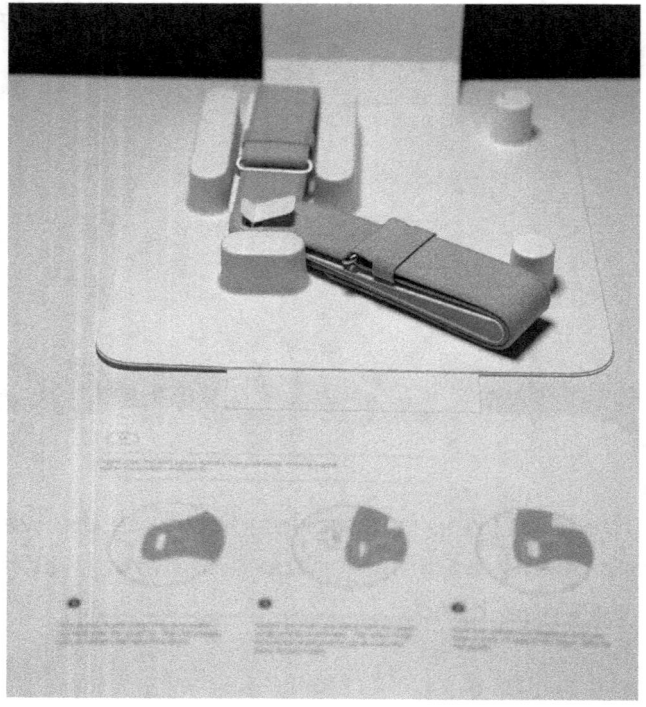

And finally, you have something not seen in and Apple Product in a very long time—something not included in most products anymore: a get started manual!

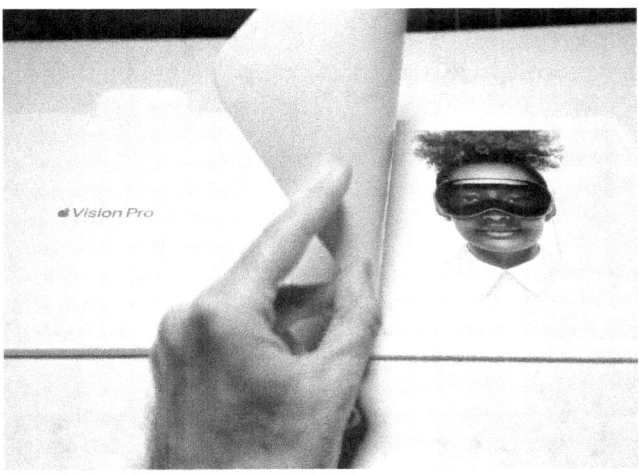

It's not at all comprehensive but covers the basics—such as removing the straps and battery; it's a very thick paper, full color and excellent quality. A part of you might want to put it on your bookshelf!

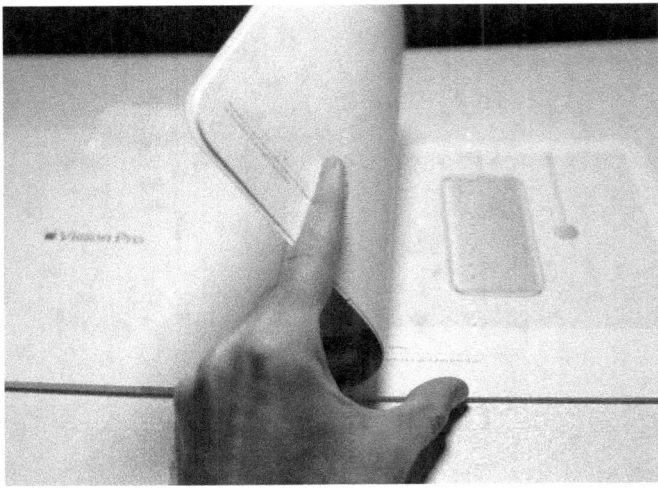

Below are a few things not included in the box, but you might want to pick up. First is the Zeiss lens inserts.

Even though this is from another company, the packaging is very much Apple, and you can tell they worked closely with Zeiss on this partnership.

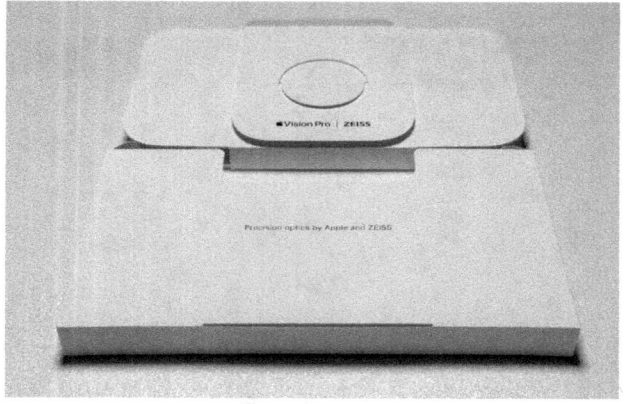

I recommend keeping the box it came in; as of this writing, there is no case for the Zeiss lens inserts; if other people use your Vision Pro, you'll have to take the inserts out and keep them somewhere that they won't get scratched.

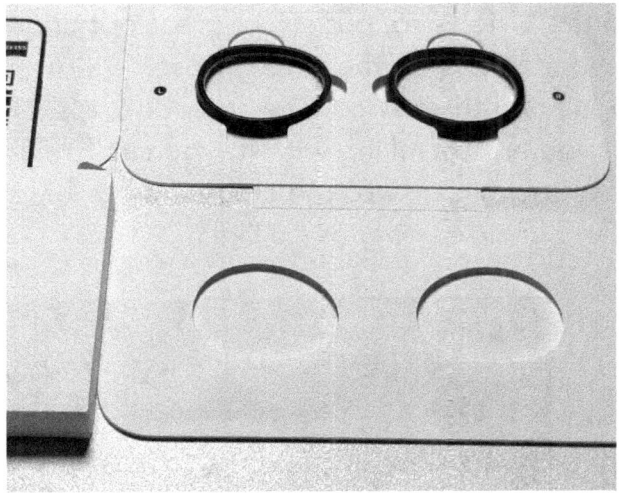

Something else I recommend buying is a spare Light Seal cushion; it's $29 and handy when someone else is using your Vision Pro. It attaches magnetically to the headset and can be swapped out in seconds.

Finally, there's the Apple Vision Pro travel case. It's $199 and one of the few cases out there, as of this option. It's your best option if you're travelling with the Vision Pro, but also a great option for storing your headset when not in use. There are two things I don't like about the case: one, it's a bit big, so if you are travelling with it, you can't really pack it in a backpack; two, the zippers are a bit stiff—it doesn't unzip as easy as I'd like.

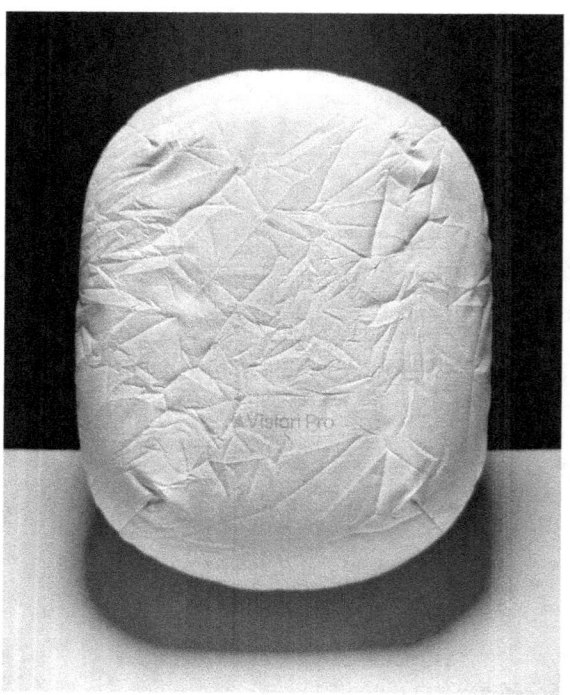

PRE-INSTALLED APPS

If you have used anything Apple (from Mac-books and iPads to iPhones) then the Vision Pro will have a lot of very familiar apps. Below are the apps that come installed with the Vision Pro. Some (like Capture and Encounter Dinosaurs) are exclusive to the Vision Pro; most are the apps you already know, but enhanced for the Vision Pro.

Apps enhanced for the Vision Pro:

- App Store
- Encounter Dinosaurs
- Files
- Freeform
- Keynote
- Mail
- Messages
- Mindfulness
- Music
- Notes
- Photos
- Safari
- Settings
- Tips
- TV

Apps installed but not optimized for the Vision Pro:

- Books
- Calendar
- Home

- Maps
- News
- Podcasts
- Reminders
- Shortcuts
- Stocks
- Voice Memos

What does installed but not optimized mean? Many apps that will be on the Vision Pro—both from developers and from Apple—will merely be iPad apps that are ported over to the Vision Pro. They work fine, but there's nothing special about them.

This book was written when the Vision Pro first came out; expect Apple to add more apps later.

[2]

GETTING STARTED

With the Vision Pro out of the box, let's take a look at using the Vision Pro for the first time.

THE BATTERY

Before you can use the Vision Pro, you have to plug it in—there is zero battery on the Vision Pro; unlike a laptop, if you unplug it, you'll still have a few hours of use, the Vision Pro will instantly shut off if you remove it.

To attach the battery, you line up the circle on the battery connector with the circle on the side of the Vision Pro (the circle that is unfilled); once it's lined up, you twist to line it up with the filled circle. To remove the battery, just follow those steps in reverse.

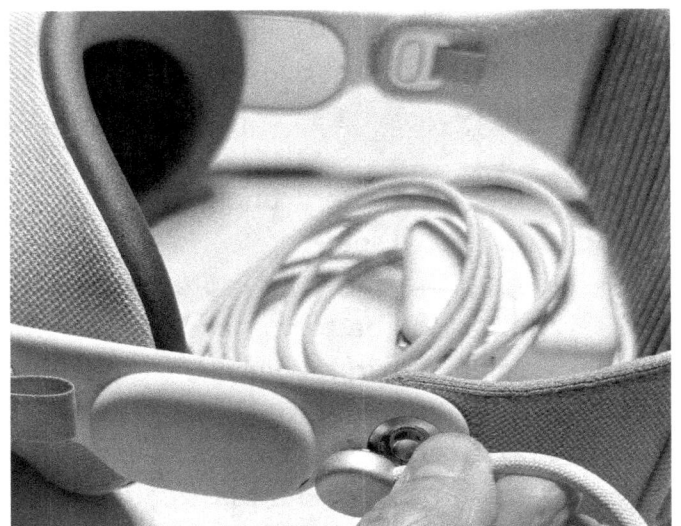

How to Charge the Apple Vision Pro Battery

The Vision Pro comes with a USB-C Charge cable and USB-C power adapter; it's recommended that you use the charging unit it came with.

What the Battery's Light Means

The battery light has different light indicators. Let's look at what they mean. If you have the charging cable plugged in, these are the different indicators:

- **Green**: the battery is full.
- **Amber**: the battery is not full, but it has enough charge for you to use Apple Vision Pro.
- **Amber blinking slowly**: the battery is too low to run your Apple Vision Pro. Charge

the battery for 10 minutes, or until the light is amber and not blinking when you tap the battery.

If you have the battery unplugged, here's the light indicators you'll see:

- **Green**: the battery is more than half full.
- **Amber**: the battery is less than half full.
- **Amber blinking slowly**: the battery is too low to run your Apple Vision Pro. Charge the battery for 10 minutes, or until the light is amber and not blinking when you tap the battery.

WEARING THE VISION PRO AND ADJUSTING THE STRAPS

Here's one of the most important things to know about getting started with the Vision Pro: it's heavy and fitting it wrong is going to make it feel heavier. Part of having a comfortable experience is adjusting the bands properly.

When I first started hearing people review the headset, I kept hearing about the weight and was a little nervous; I wanted this for productivity and to work while I wasn't in my office. How was I going to do that with a brick on my head?!

To my relief, it was a little lighter than expected; even better, adjusting the straps really does help.

The Vision Pro comes with two headbands (and the headbands come in different sizes): the Solo Knit

Band and the Dual Loop Band. The Solo Knit Band is already attached to your Vision Pro, but you can switch to the Dual Loop Band anytime you want. Just take off the Solo Knit Band and snap on the Dual Loop Band.

Most people will probably find the weight is distributed more evenly with the Dual Loop Band, which goes over the head, but my advice is try both for a little bit of time.

WEARING THE VISION PRO WITH THE SOLO KNIT BAND

Grab your device by the frame with one hand and the Solo Knit Band with the other. Don't pick up Vision Pro by the Light Seal, Straps, or power cable; these can come loose and cause you to drop the Vision Pro.

Put the device close to your face and slide the Solo Knit Band over the back of your head. Depending on your hairstyle, you might find it easier to put the head band on first and then pull the device over your eyes.

Once you have the device on, turn the Fit Dial clockwise to make the Solo Knit Band tighter and counterclockwise to make it looser. You want the Vision Pro to be snug. You can also move the back higher or lower to see if it distributes the weight better.

When I bought the Vision Pro, it said to get the medium; I ended up getting the small as well to be safe, and found that the small was more comfortable. So if you don't like how it feels, it could be you have the wrong strap size.

If your headband is too tight, it might irritate your skin, make you feel uncomfortable, or leave marks on your face. The marks will go away pretty quick.

If your headband is too loose or not in the right position, you probably will see a message that says that the device is too high or too low. Just move it up or down until it feels right.

WEARING VISION PRO WITH THE DUAL LOOP BAND

Pick up the device, and again, remember to hold your Vision Pro by the frame, and not the Light Seal, straps or cable.

Put the device close to your face and slide the Dual Loop Band over the back of your head.

Hold Vision Pro to your face with one hand, making sure it's evenly supported on your forehead and cheeks.

While you're holding Vision Pro to your face, use your other hand to tighten the lower strap first, then the upper strap.

REMOVING THE STRAP

To remove the strap, hold the headset with one hand, and with the other, pull upward on the orange tab; it slides off easily. To put it back in, just slide it in.

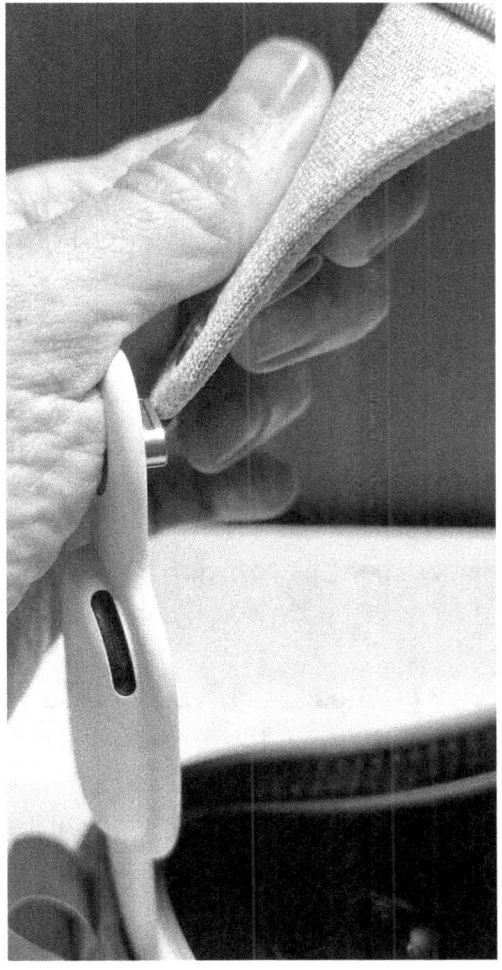

How to take off Apple Vision Pro

Make the headband looser before you take it off. For the Solo Knit Band, just turn the Fit Dial to the left. For the Dual Loop Band, just pull the tab on the lower strap away from your head.

Take off the device by holding the frame.

When you put down your device, don't let the cover glass touch any hard surfaces, like a table or countertop. They might scratch it. Put the battery next to Vision Pro when you're not using it so the power cable doesn't get tangled with other stuff.

When you're done with Vision Pro, put the cover on to keep it safe.

HOW TO MAKE VISION PRO FIT PERFECTLY

As much as possible, you want the Vision Pro to feel balanced on your face. It should be snug, but not tight.

If the head band is too tight, turn the Fit Dial to the left and pull the device by the frame away from your face.

If your eyelashes touch your Vision Pro or your eyes are too far away, then you will see a message that your eyes are too close to the screens; try using the Light Seal Cushion with a "+" on it that came in your box. If that doesn't work, you might need a different size Light Seal.

CLEANING

Cleaning is an important part of keeping your Vision Pro working as intended. Dirty or smudgy cameras, for example, might affect how hand tracking work.

First: **don't** use isopropyl alcohol, Windex, Clorox, or similar stuff to clean surfaces of the Vision Pro. Clean your Vision Pro with a dry cloth, a little wet cloth, or ideally, the cloth that came with the Vision pro.

Make sure your Apple Vision Pro Polishing Cloth is clean and keep it in a clean bag. Backpacks, handbags, pockets, and other places might have things that could scratch your device.

CLEANING THE GLASS COVER

If the cover glass gets dirty, wipe it with a clean, dry microfiber cloth — like the one that came with your Apple Vision Pro.

If you see any loose things on your cover glass, wipe them with a clean, dry microfiber cloth.

THE SETUP

The Vision Pro setup is very easy; unfortunately, I could not capture it, but I'll do my best to explain the steps below:

Step 1

Place the headband on your head and turn the dial on the right side of the headband to adjust the fit. The display will tell you to press and hold the digital crown and gaze at the floating glasses to adjust your view.

Step 2

You need an iPhone or iPad to set up the Vision Pro. The headset will ask you to bring your phone close to your face and unlock it. Your phone will display a QR code that you need to scan with the headset to continue.

Step 3

Hand gestures are the first main way you'll interact with VisionOS, so the headset needs to recognize your hands. It will ask you to extend your arms in front of you and show your palms to the headset. Then it will ask you to turn your hands over.

Step 4

Eye tracking is the second way you'll be interacting with your environment, so the headset needs to track how your eyes move. It will ask you to look at a dot, then at six dots in a circle, and tap your finger as you look at each one. Then it will brighten the screen and do the circle again, then brighten it more and do it one last time.

Step 5

You can skip this step if you want and do it later. I'll show you how in the book. The Vision Pro will ask you to remove it and point the Vision Pro at your face. The display on the front will glow and show you some circles with your face in them. The speakers will ask you to look at the headset, then tilt your head left, right, up, and down. Then it will record your facial expressions by asking you to smile with your mouth closed, smile with your teeth, close your eyes, and raise your eyebrows. These eight actions are enough for the Vision Pro to create what's called a Persona—I'll cover this a bit more later.

This was the most frustrating part of the setup for me. The first time I tried it, it kept telling me to look down and left, then it said the setup failed. The second time I tried with better lighting, and it succeeded. It should be noted, that this feature is in Beta.

Step 6

The Vision Pro uses Optic ID instead of Face ID. This means it scans your eyes to confirm your identity—that way you don't have to type in your password. After you set up your FaceTime persona, the Vision Pro will ask you to look at a symbol. After a few seconds, Optic ID will be set. That's it. As a backup, the Vision Pro will also ask you to set up a six-digit passcode (you can also switch it to four-digit). You'll need to use the passcode whenever the Vision Pro restarts.

If you lose your passcode you will have to bring the headset to an Apple Store to recover it, so make sure you pick something you remember.

Step 7

You're almost there. The the Vision Pro will show you a quick tutorial on how to use the basic gestures and functions, like selecting items, resizing windows, and opening quick menus.

That's it. You're all set. The whole process is very easy, but it takes about 10 minutes. I didn't show you here how to set up the Zeiss inserts. You can do that during the setup or later. I'll show you how in the book.

USING VISION PRO WITH ZEISS INSERTS

If you didn't add your Zeiss inserts during the setup, you can quickly do it at any time after you start using the device by following these steps.

With the on the Vision Pro, attach the optical inserts; they'll snap right in—just make sure you are snapping them into the correct side.

Remove the cover, then put on the Vision Pro. It will automatically detect the inserts and walk you through the setup process; part of the process will be scanning a code that came with your inserts, so make sure you don't through away the box!

You can also pair new inserts at any time, by going to Settings > Eyes & Hands, and then tapping on Setup Up New Optical Inserts.

[3]

NAVIGATING AROUND THE VISION PRO

Now that you've learned what the Vision Pro is (and isn't) and seen what the setup is like, let's learn how to move around the device.

GESTURES

Before getting into the OS itself, let's talk about gestures.

Gestures are probably the first thing that will completely blow you away when you use the Vision Pro; yes, it's a stunning display and the apps can be addictively fun. But it's really how sophisticated the gestures are that reveal how much tech is inside this thing. It's intuitive and when you get used to it, it's faster than using a mouse.

Before I go into the different gestures, here are a few things to keep in mind:

- It may seem like some kind of magic, but it's actually all the cameras that make gestures work; that means you need to keep the cameras clean and have enough light for the cameras to see you. If it's having difficulty registering what your hands are doing, it could be you need more light or the camera is dirty.
- You don't have to lift your arm up when you use Apple Vision Pro. You can keep your hand relaxed on your desk or in your lap when making most gestures. The first time, your hands will probably instinctively raise up, but just remember that they don't have to.
- Make sure Apple Vision Pro can see your hands, and not hide them under a desk or a blanket.
- If you wear gloves, it's probably not going to read your gestures–if it does, it's not going to be as accurate.
- Don't cross your hands. It won't know you're right from your left.

So let's look at the gestures:

Touch

You can touch some things in visionOS directly with your fingers. For example, when the visionOS virtual keyboard shows up, you can type by touching the keys directly with one finger on each hand.

Tap your fingers together

To pick something in Apple Vision Pro, look at it and tap your thumb and index finger together.

Tapping your thumb and index finger together is like tapping something on your iPhone or clicking something on your computer — use this gesture to pick an app.

Pinch to see more options

Pinch and hold something in Apple Vision Pro to see more options. Look at something, tap your thumb and index finger together, and hold. When you see more options, let go and then tap to pick the option you want.

Pinch and drag

To move things around in Apple Vision Pro, look at something and then pinch your thumb and index finger together. Keep your thumb and finger together as you move it where you want it, then let go. This can be things like Windows or menus.

Pinch and flick your wrist

To move or scroll fast through stuff, pinch your thumb and index finger together, flick your wrist up or down, then let go in one smooth move.

BUTTONS

The Vision Pro has two buttons:

1. **The Digital Crown** that controls the amount of the environment that is showing and brings up the Home button
2. **The Top button**, which is what you use to take photos—it's the one on the left side of the headset.

The buttons can also be used for another of shortcuts, as you can see below.

SCREENSHOTS

I'll show you how to do screen recording in the section on Control Center; if you want to capture a still screenshot of your screen press the Digital Crown and Top button at the same time. You'll hear a camera sound and the screen capture will be stored in your library.

FORCE CRASH APP

If an app isn't responding Press and Hold the Top button and Digital Crown at the same time until a window comes up asking you what you want to force close.

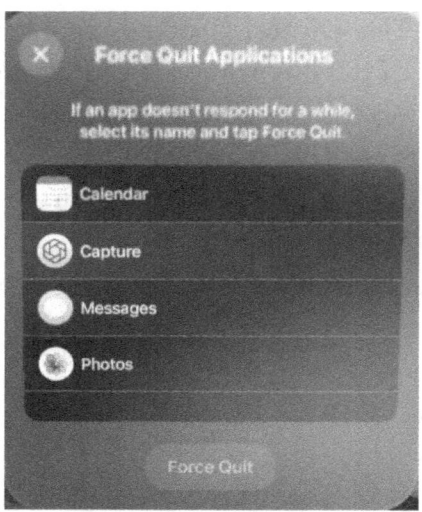

POWER VISION PRO OFF

There is no power button on the Vision Pro, but you can still power it down. Do the same steps as above (press and hold the Digital Crown and Top button), but continue to hold longer. A message will come up to power the Vision Pro off.

RECALIBRATE TRACKING

If you want to recalibrate your vision tracking, press the Top button 5 times.

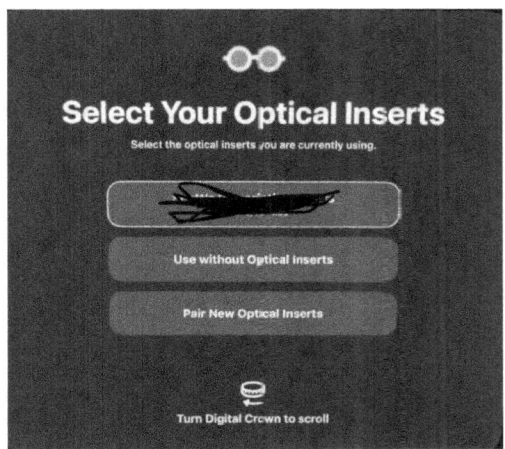

GUIDED ACCESS

Guided Access is an accessibility featured that you can turn on by triple pressing the Digital Crown. With Guided Access, you can lock your Vision Pro to one app only, and choose what you can do in that app. This way, you won't get distracted by other stuff.

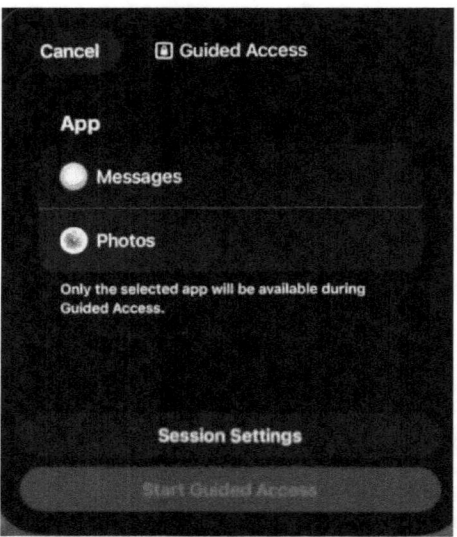

TYPING

There are a few ways to type on the Vision Pro:

1. With the virtual keyboard - this works one of two ways: one, you look at a letter and pinch to select it; or two, you one handed type by pressing the letter. This works pretty well, but it's definitely the slower of the two methods.

2. Speak to text – This is going to be the fastest way for most people. When the keyboard comes up, just select the microphone and say what you want the text to say.

3. Use a Bluetooth keyboard – this is by far the best and fastest method, but that means you also have to bring a keyboard along if you are traveling.

MOVING, RESIZING, AND CLOSING WINDOWS

There's one final thing to cover before we jump into an overview of the OS: Resize, Move, and Close apps.

RESIZE WINDOWS

If you look in the corner of any window, you'll see a curved line on the edge of the window. You can pinch your fingers and move them in or out ot resize the window.

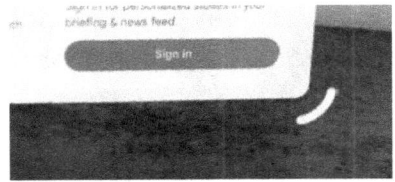

MOVE AND CLOSE APPS

To move an app use the line on the bottom edge of any window. To close the app, tap on the circle next to that line (which will turn to an X when you hover over it.

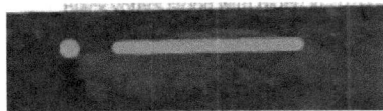

If you are in an immersive environment, look for back buttons—typically in the upper left corner. If all else fails, use the Force Close shortcut (Press and Hold the Top button and Digital Crown at the same time)

MAIN HOME SCREEN AND NAVIGATION

Let's start learning about the OS behind the headset. I'll do my best to take screenshots that are clean and even, but because of the nature of the device, things aren't always as clear as screenshots on iOS and iPadOS. That's because the way Vision Pro works is it focus on what you're looking at—you don't notice it because of how our eyes work, but you'll see it when you take screenshots. So don't let the images fool you—it's much sharper when it's on your eyes.

The first time you finish setup, you'll see three rows of apps. This is your Home screen. It's very iPad / iPhone like isn't it? You'll find many similarities between visionOS and iOS, iPadOS, and even macOS and watchOS.

A few things you should know about the Home screen:

- The first group of apps are the ones created by Apple.
- Apps are arranged alphabetically (Except for the Apple built ones, which are always the first to show up).
- Apps cannot be arranged or grouped (except for the folder for "compatible apps" which are apps that came over from iOS or iPadOS.

These constraints are not a deal-breaker, but they are annoying, and it won't take you long for you to complain to yourself about wanting it to work differently. Most likely a future update will address this.

Here's the other thing you should know about the Home menu: pressing the digital crown will recenter the Home screen. So if you turn and want the home screen in the new place, just press the digital crown.

Over on the left side is the Home menu. There's three things there: Apps, People, and Environments.

Apps is the menu that was show above. People is your favorite contacts. You can use the + to add or find someone—this is also how you would make a FaceTime call. Just open the contact and tap FaceTime.

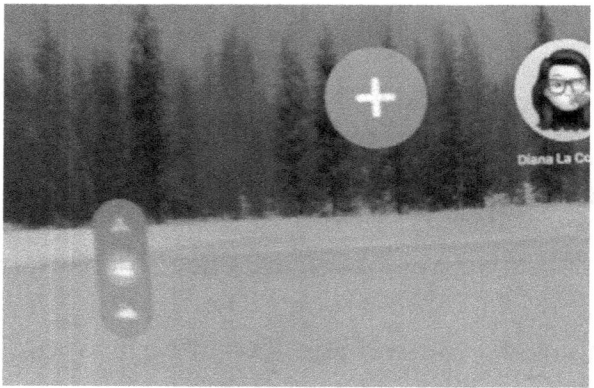

Environments is one of the coolest features of the headset, in my opinion. It lets you change your surroundings into an immersive environment. So you can feel like you are working at the beach or in the mountains. It really does feel life like.

Available Environments

Below is a list of all available environments with more coming soon:

- Haleakalā
- Yosemite
- Joshua Tree
- Mount Hood
- The Moon
- Beach
- White Sands
- Winter Light
- Fall Light
- Summer Light
- Spring Light

Removing Apps

You can remove an app by tapping and holding on the app you want to remove. It will delete it from the Vision Pro, but it can still be downloaded again from the app store at no cost.

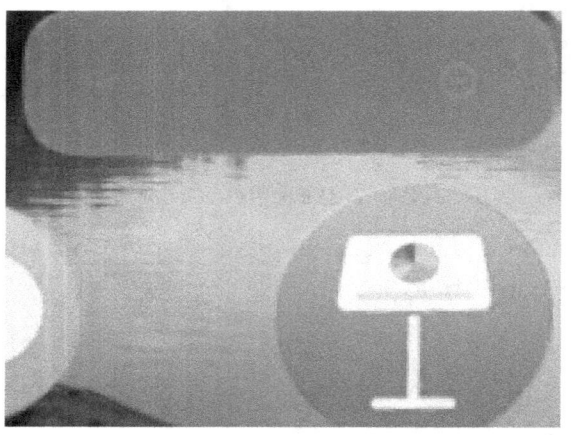

Using the Digital Crown

When you select an environment, you can use the Digital Crown to adjust how immersive it is. The more you turn the more immersive it is. Turning it all the way back will turn it off. Turning it all the way on will make the environment fill everything—look up, down, left and right and you'll see it. Even cooler, if you turn it all the way on, you even hear what it sounds like.

Depending on the time of day, your environment will also be light or dark; you can adjust that in Control Center, which I'll cover next.

What's really crazy about being in these immersive environments is when someone talks to you, it will automatically begin to fade out so you can see them! (that's a setting you can turn off) You can remove them by turning the dial again.

CONTROL CENTER

Control Center can be accessed at anytime by looking up. You'll see a very small box—so small you might even miss it! Just tap on it to get started.

This will bring up a box with four icons and a volume slider. The first icon takes you back to the Home screen. The second icon is for environments. This will bring up the menu to change your environments—if you want Dark or Automatic mode, for example.

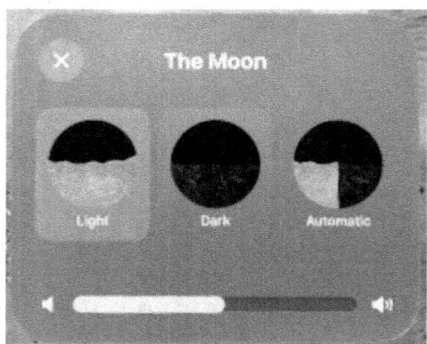

The last option (we'll come back to the third momentarily) is the Notification Center; mine is empty, but if I had any, then they'd show up here.

And finally, the third icon brings up Control Center. Control Center, just like on the iPhone or iPad, is where all your control shortcuts live.

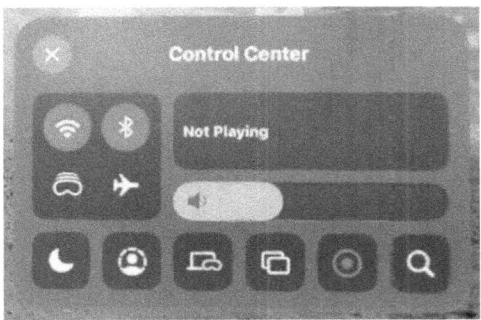

The first four icons will toggle things on and off. You probably know that first is to turn off Wi-Fi and the one next to it turns off Bluetooth; and your probably familiar with the plane, which represents Airplane mode. But what's going on with that icon that looks like the Vision Pro? That's travel mode. It's made for when you are *flying*. It emphasize flying because this is not for when your driving or anything else—Apple specifies that it's only for when you're flying; they also say to stop using it during turbulence. When in travel mode, the Vision Pro works to stabilize your experience.

Now playing shows you what (if anything) is currently playing on your Vision Pro; the volume slider under it will control how loud or soft it is.

Next, let's look at those bottom six icons. The first one puts it into different focus mode. This will pause notifications for a set amount of time.

The second icon is Guest Mode. You'll probably have a lot of requests for this one. This is for when a person says, "Hey! Is that a Vision Pro?! Can I try it?!"

When you press Guest Mode, you'll be asked what the person can see. Guest Mode isn't like handing over an iPad with all your features enabled. Guest Mode lets you decide what a user can and can't see.

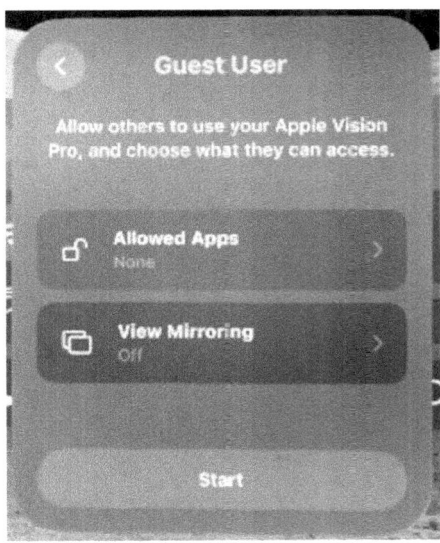

From Allowed Apps, you can decide if the user will see everything or only the apps that you've opened up for them.

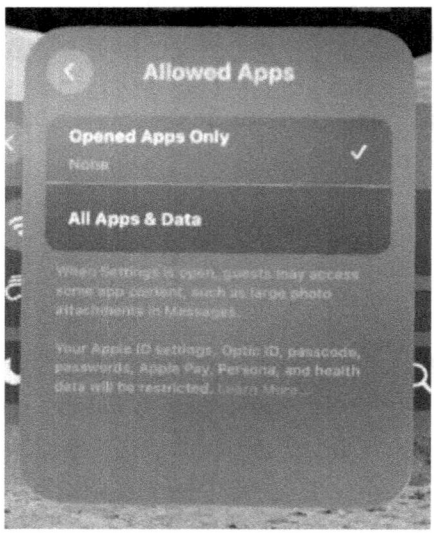

Once you press the start button, the person will have five minutes to start there session; they'll have to go through a setup process that will take a couple minutes (and no, unfortunately, this cannot be saved.

There's one other cool feature to consider before handing it over: View Mirroring. When you select this, you can mirror the Vision Pro to either a compatible iPad or Mac, so you can watch what they're doing and help them if they get stuck.

The next icon I'll go a little deeper into later in the book, but this is to bring a Mac to ycur Vision Pro.

Just make sure it's close and on the same network.

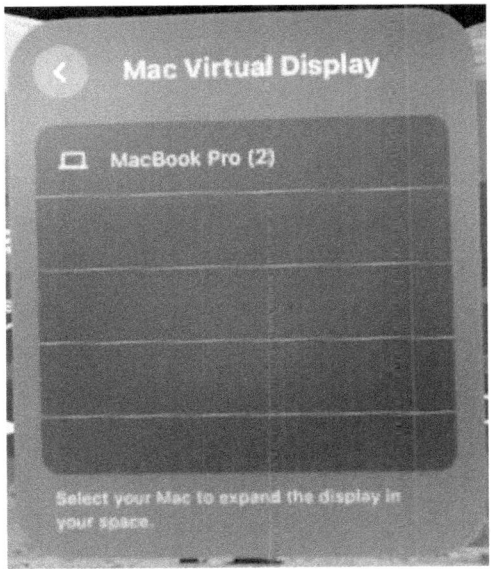

The next icon lets you mirror your Vision Pro to a compatible AirPlay device so others can see what you see.

I mentioned earlier in this chapter how to screen-shot a screen. This option takes that up a notch by letting you do a screen recording.

Finally, the last option is the Search, which helps you quickly find apps and documents on your Vision Pro.

So now you know the basics of the Vision Pro. It's really intuitive, so you'll be surprised at how fast much you know without even knowing it. Next, we'll take a look at all the main apps on the Vision Pro.

CONNECTING TO A MAC

Connecting to a Mac can be done one of two ways; the first is through the Control Center (mentioned above); the second, and quicker way, is by looking at your Mac.

You read that right! Just look at your Mac and Vision Pro will know what you mean. Above your Mac display, it will have the option to connect.

For the most part, I found this to work pretty well. But there were times when it didn't show up; and then I went to Control Center and it didn't show up.

It's not a lost cause. If I went to my Control Center on my Macbook, and click Screen Mirroring, my Visio Pro showed up.

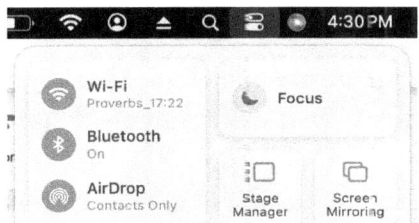

Once I clicked that, it showed up on my display in seconds. So it wasn't always perfect; but once it was there, it worked exactly as I hoped—in beautiful 4K.

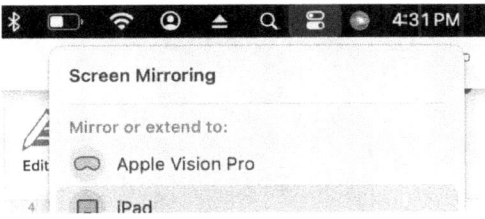

Vision Pro is an innovative device that might someday replace our computers and even offices, but it still has some limitations. Here are a few things to keep in mind—and hopefully these will be improved over time:

- You can only connect one Mac at a time. I have one for home and one for work, and it would be convenient to have them in the same space together.

- You only get one monitor. You can create multiple windows, but they are all on the same screen. Yes, your screen is massive—but you might still want to drag things out of your computer and into your environment.

- If you don't use your Mac's keyboard and mouse, you might have a hard time navigating. I hide my dock, and I couldn't find a way to reveal it without using the trackpad.

- Your workspace isn't saved when you turn off your Vision Pro. I organized everything nicely—clock up here, Teams over here, Slack to the other side; and then I turned off the device for the day. When I turned it back on, I had to reorganize everything. This doesn't happen if you put it on standby.

- When scrolling, I sometimes experienced a lag—it scrolled too slowly.

You have to remember that this is a Day One product. It will get better and better. For me, I found that some tasks in Vision Pro made me more productive. For others—like writing—I still preferred not using it.

That said, here is one thing I had less of: neck strain. I like to use my laptop on my lap, which means

I look down a lot. With the Vision Pro, I found my neck was more aligned even though I was in a relaxed position. Some people complain about the weight of it, but personally, I barely notice it and have no problem using it for long periods of time.

I've also used the Meta Quest 3 for work. I can't say the same for that experience. It was a hassle to connect my Mac; the picture wasn't clear; and I felt I was getting less done.

[4]

THE APPS

On day one, the Vision Pro had about 600 apps build just for visionOS; that sounds like a lot, but considering iPad has over a million, that number suddenly seems smaller. But here's the good news: one, and most importantly, most iPad apps are compatible with visionOS, and, as long as the developer didn't disable it, it will be in the store (the reason you don't see apps like Netflix, Spotify, and YouTube isn't because they aren't compatible—it's because they were disabled by the companies).

The other good news is developers seem to be really excited about developing for the Vision Pro and pushing the limits of what it can do.

Finally, the apps that are already on the Vision Pro are good. This book will cover the Apple installed apps, but there are plenty more on the app store to pick from.

APPLE TV

Apple TV is the first icon you'll see on your Home menu; it's probably going to be one of your favorites because this is where most the 3D movies live. It also has the best movie watching experience. Disney+ let's you change the environment, but Apple TV lets you change the seat position.

The Apple TV menu on the left side is broken up into seven options:

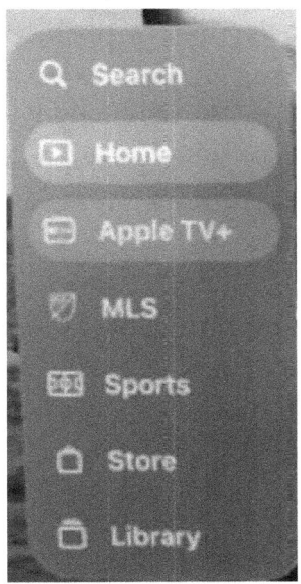

- **Search** – The first option lets you search for all your media content—you can also search for genres or even formats (like 3D)

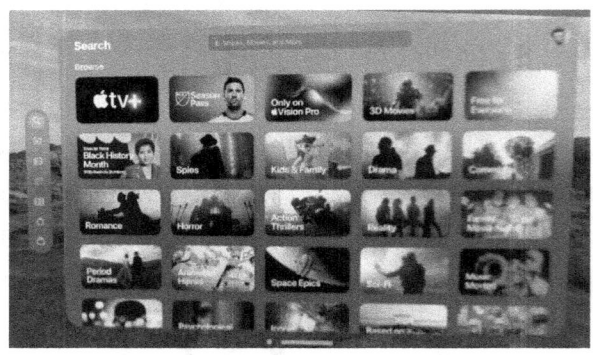

- **Home** – The main Home area of the app is Apple's attempt to make media watching easier; below promos for content, you'll see Up Next which is recommendations for what they think you'll watch next based on what you've watched in the past; so if there's a new TV show that you are known to watch, it will show up here. And not just a TV show on Apple TV—it could be on Peacock, Max or virtually anywhere else.

- **Apple TV+** - This is where Apple has been spending a lot of it's money. It's underappreciated, in my opinion; it may not have as much as Netflix or Disney+, but the content that is here is good—some of the best stuff on TV. If you've never tried shows like *For All Mankind*, then it's the perfect time—and it's a show that's made for this type of viewing..

- **MLS** – Apple has a contract with MLS and the content will show here.

- **Sports** – Apple has been working on several sports licenses that will show up here.

- **Store** – Apple has previously had sold movies and TV shows through the iTunes app; that went away a few months before Vision Pro launched. Now anything you want to buy is in the Apple TV app.

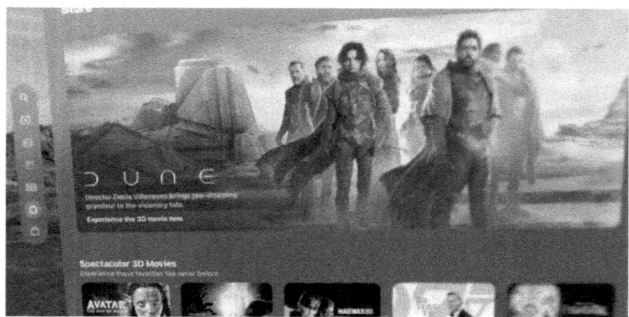

- **Library** – Whenever you buy something (or anything you've bought in the past) will show up here. One of the best things: content you've bought in the past that is available in 3D is free to you; so if you bought Avatar a few years ago in the regular format, it's now upgraded to 3D.

VIEWING MOVIES

In this section, I'll show you what the Apple TV viewing interface looks like; unfortunately, no movie is showing do to copyright.

On the top portion of the screen is the back icon (to exit a movie) the environment icon, and the volume icon. On the bottom is the forward 10, pause, back 10 seconds, and extra options.

The extra options are for Playback Speed, Languages, Subtitles, and Auto Dimming (if you're watching a movie while working, then you can uncheck this).

When you click on Environments, you can select if you want to stay in your environment or move things into a cinema. The Cinema environment is where things get really cool.

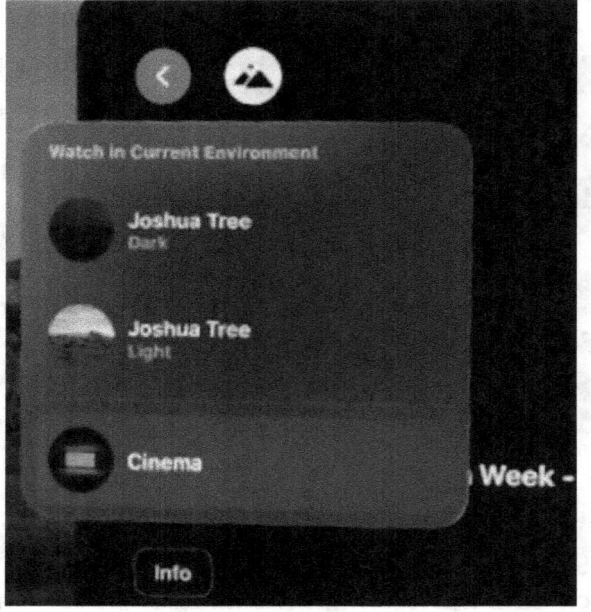

When you select Cinema, you can select the row you want to sit in (front, middle, back) and how high up you are (floor or balcony).

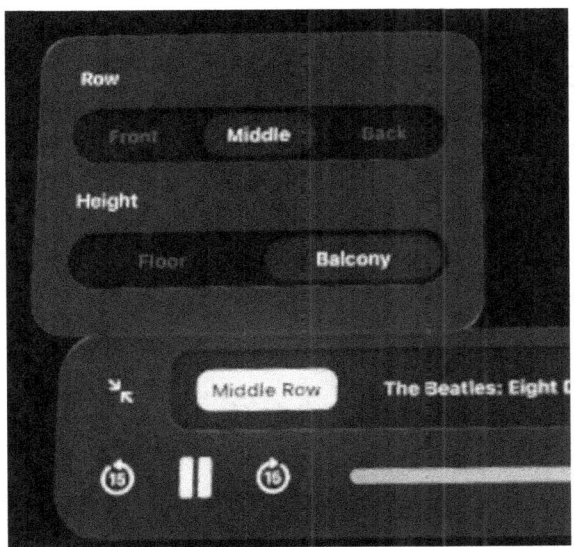

MUSIC

There may not be a Spotify app on the Vision Pro (yet), but Apple has included their own rival app and if you are already invested in the Apple ecosystem, you definitely should check it out; personally, my house has the Apple One service that includes Apple Music, TV, Arcade, News, and Fitness; it's a great service if you enjoy Apple.

Apple Music currently starts at $10.99 ($5.99 for students); Apple One currently starts at $19.95; each service goes up in price depending on what you get—family or non-family for example, or if you want something like Fitness+ (which, unfortunately, is not included as a Vision Pro app at this time).

Let's take a look at what Apple Music looks like on the Vision Pro.

Vision Pro apps have adopted a pretty standard design pattern where menus go on the left side. So anytime you want to view menus, start by looking on the left.

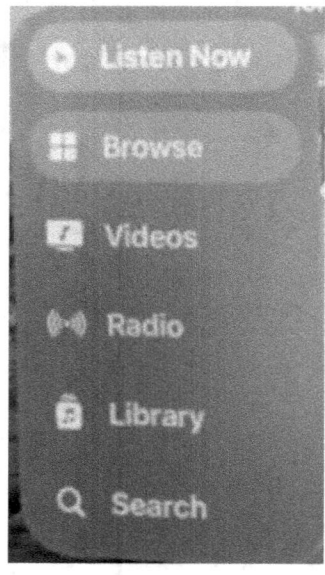

The menu bar on the Vision Pro locks a lot like the options available on iPad and iPhone—this is something you'll hear a lot in this book because Apple has intentionally tried to make the experience as similar as possible, which makes it remarkably easy to pick up if you're already familiar with iOS or iPadOS.

The options on the Menu are:

- **Listen Now** – this is the main area and is like the homepage for recommendations and recently played.

- **Browse** – Let's you see music by different categories / genres and recommendations; if you want to hear music in Spatial audio (a format that takes advantage of the Vision Pro's speakers), you'll find it in here.

- **Videos** – This space is devoted to music videos.

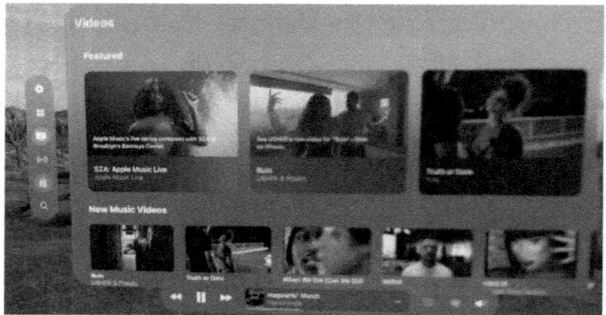

- **Radio** – If you don't know what you are looking for, the Radio area has different commercial free stations in several different genres that is curated by Apple.

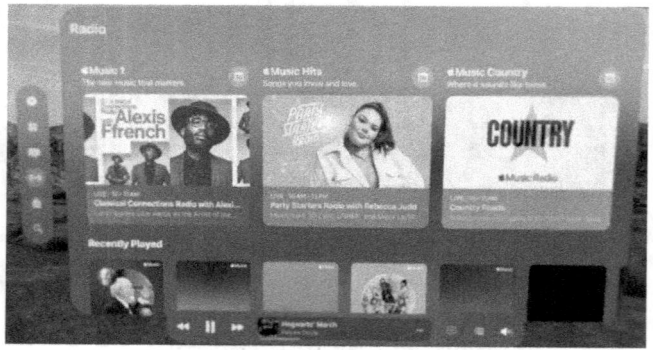

- **Library** – If you own any music, you'll see it here. This is also where you'll find your playlists.

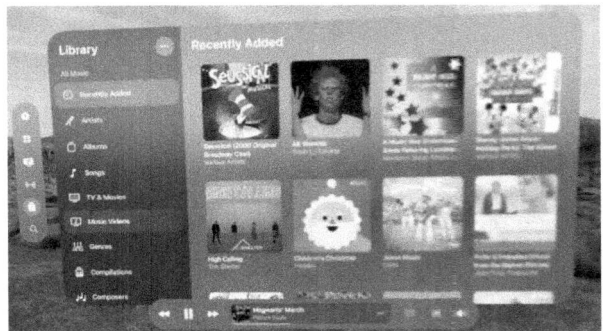

- **Search** – Search lets you search for different artist and genres.

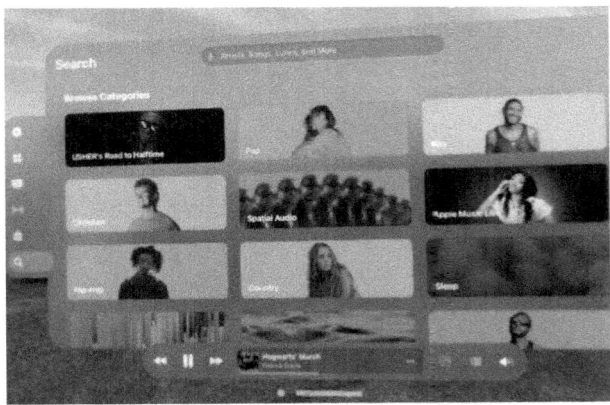

PLAYING MUSIC

When you play music, it will show up in the bottom bar; there's a few options as it plays.

Tapping the three dots, for example, will let you add it to your library, create a station, and more.

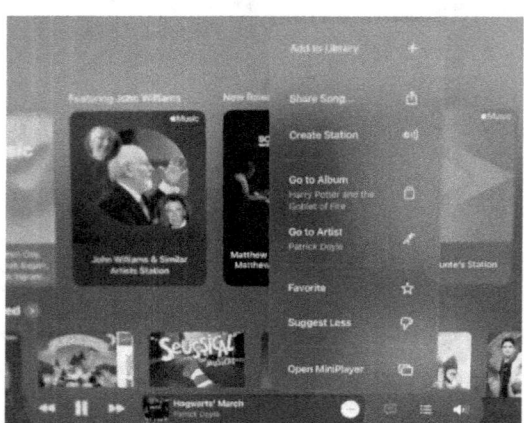

Tapping on the song will let you see the album or artist.

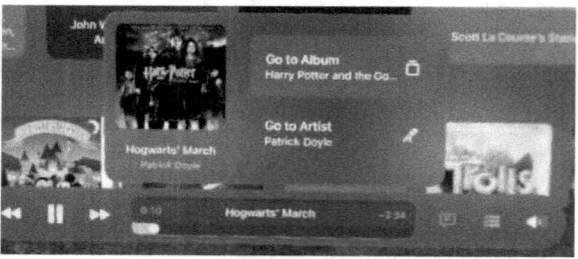

MINDFULNESS

One of the things that Apple promoted when it showed off the Vision Pro was mediation. In many ways, it's the perfect experience for Vision Pro, because the headset can be so...isolating.

If you feel like you just need to unwind, the Mindfulness is Apple's solution. It's beautiful in its simplicity.

When you open the app, it asks you how long you want to do it, then it says starts. That's it. Like I said: it's very simplistic.

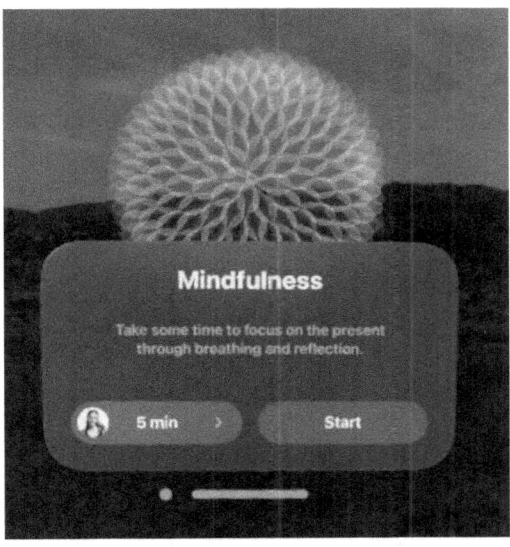

If you tap the number of minutes, it will give you the option to change both the time and the instructor. There's also a self-guided option if you want to do it on your own.

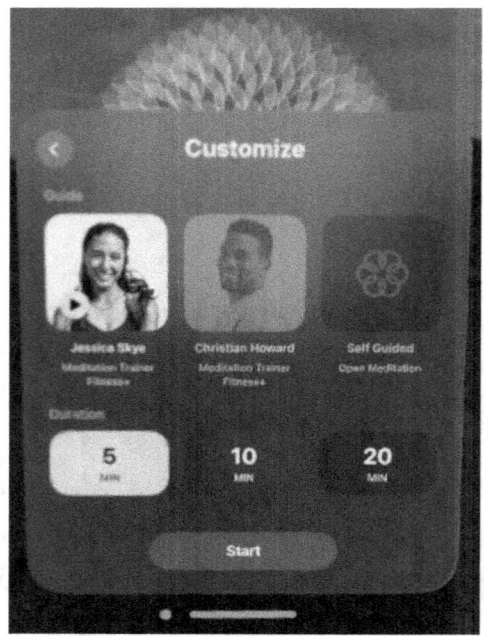

As the meditation goes, you'll see a ball going in and out to help you visualize your breathing.

After the mediation is finished, you can add information to track your session.

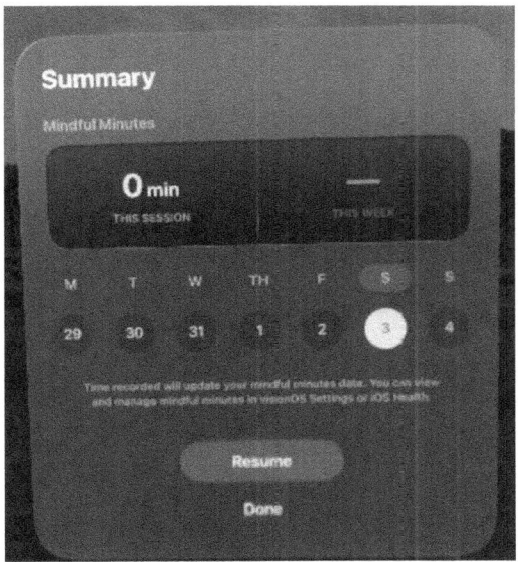

FREEFORM

Freeform was launched on Mac and iPadOS a few years ago, but Vision Pro might just be where it was ultimately destined to be. Freeform is a digital whiteboard that is ideal for collaboration.

The controls are very simple. On the bottom of the screen are all your options. There are several sets of markets, and each one can have a different color.

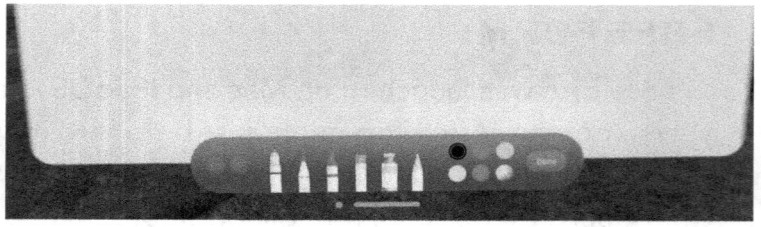

You can pinch and drag your finger across the screen to write (or scribble in my example) with the selected pen.

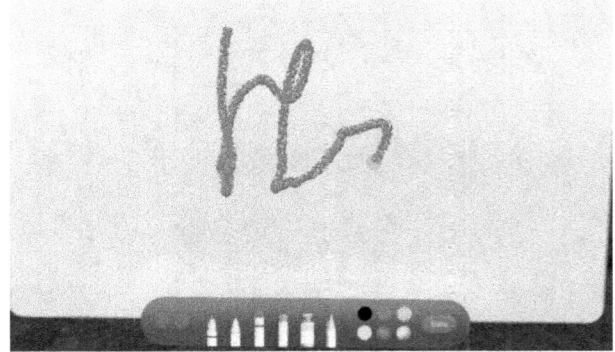

There's also objects that you can add in; you can drag the corners in and out to resize them. You can also add text.

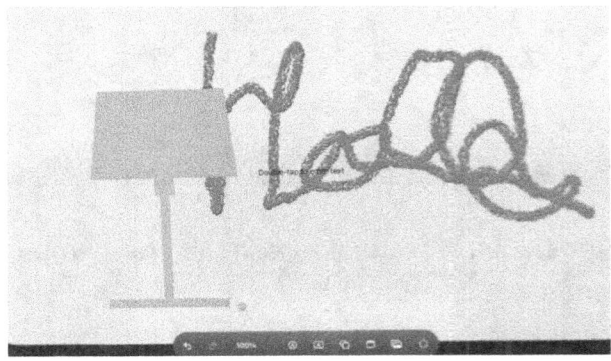

And there's sticky notes you can put every-where.

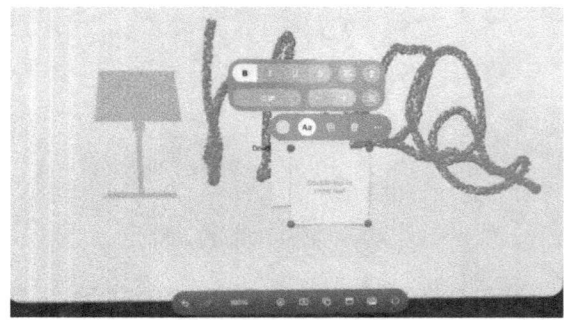

You can, of course, add images too.

Once you're done, you can tap the name up top to rename it or export it.

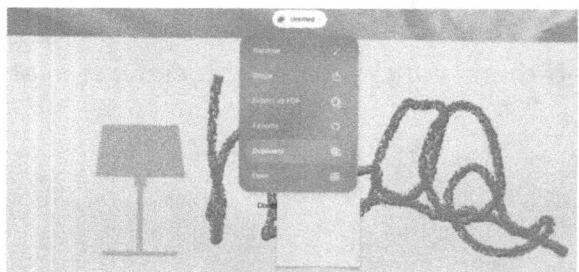

SAFARI

Safari is the main way you'll browse the Internet. As of this writing, it's your best bet if you want a native Vision Pro app. Firefox is available as a compatible app.

Hovering int his top section will reveal the tabs that you have open. Pressing the + icon will open a new tab.

You can reveal all your tabs by tapping the last icon to the right side—it looks like two pieces of paper stacked together.

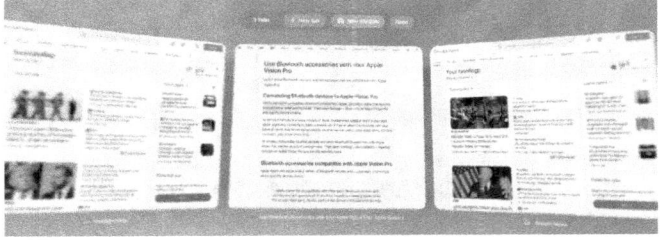

Pressing the AA icon will show you all the page options for what you are looking at.

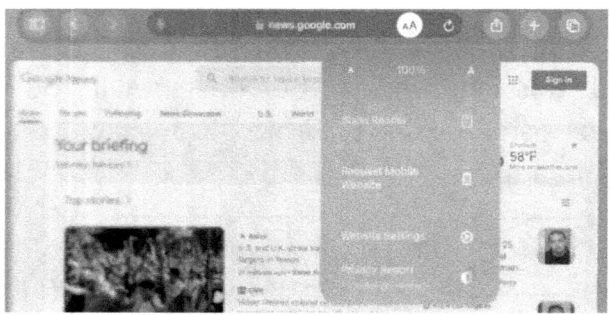

PRIVATE VIEWING

To view a page privately (meaning your history isn't tracked, tap the icon to the far left to reveal the side bar, then select the Private option. When you open a new tab, it will be in private mode. To get back to regular mode just tap the one above with the Vision Pro icon.

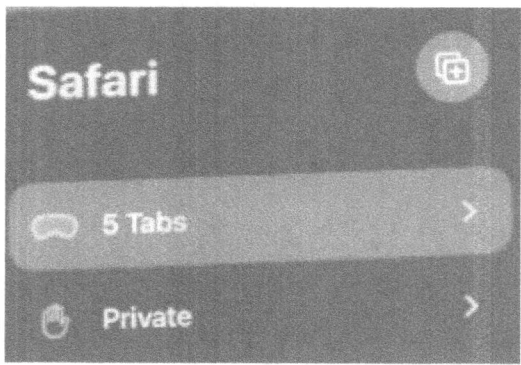

NOTES

Notes has also been optimized for Vision Pro, but it looks almost exactly the same.

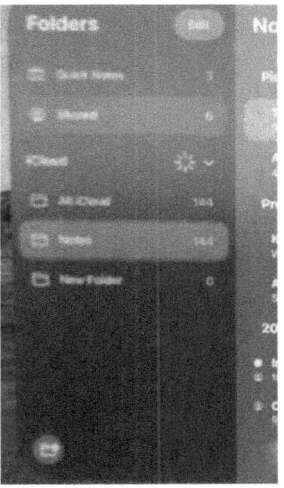

MAIL

Checking email on the Vision Pro can be done on the Web, but if you want to do it natively, your stuck with either getting a compatible app designed for iPad, or using Apple's Mail app. It looks very familiar to Mail on any other Apple product. When you open it up, you can add your email; you do have the option after you add one account, to add more. So you can have multiple mail accounts.

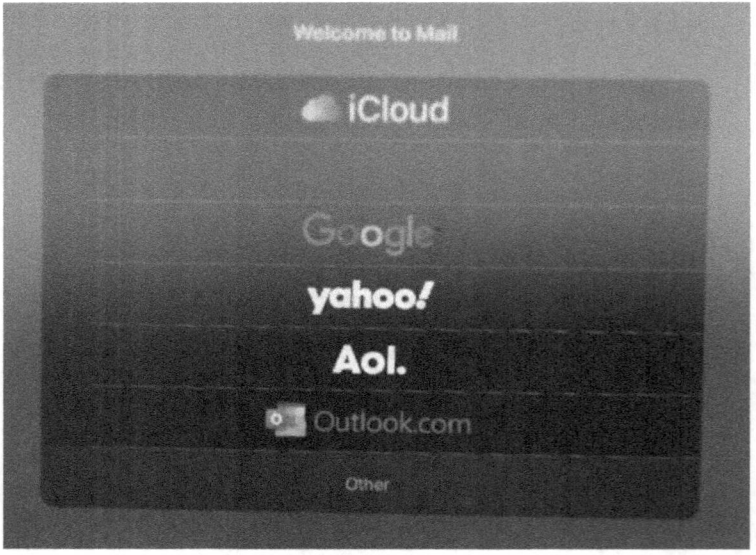

MESSAGES

Messages looks almost identical to iPad, but it is optimized for Vision Pro.

KEYNOTE

Keynote is the only iWork app included on the Vision Pro (though iPad apps of the others are supported.

When you see, I think you'll understand why. Pages and Numbers work just fine as iPad apps; I'm sure at some point they'll be optimized for Vision Pro, and they'll be a little more useful when they are. But Keynote was truly build for the Vision Pro, and, in my opinion, gives one of the best glimpses into the future of this type computing. It shows what might ultimately become one of the greatest use cases of Vision Pro: education.

The app itself is similar to Keynote on Mac or iPad; so if you've used it there, you'll be fine using it here. This isn't a comprehensive guide on how to use the apps, so I won't go into all the features here, but there's one in particular that I want to highlight: doing presentations.

When you select practice a presentation, you are giving the option of rehearsing in either a conference room or the Steve Jobs auditorium!

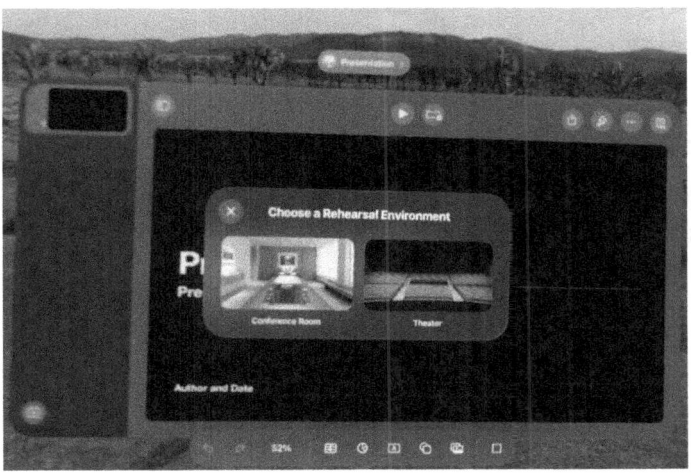

In both setups, you have your slides previewed in front of you, and when you turn behind you, you see your presentation. It really feels like your standing on stage presenting to an empty room, and there behind you is what your empty audience sees.

It's cool, but why is it a glimpse into the future? Vision Pro is at day one; think about the future—think about those kids in elementary school right now who will probably be packing a Vision Pro when they go away for college. Except back up: will they really need to go away to college anymore?

What if what we see here is presenter mode, but in the future there's a "viewer mode"? A mode that lets you step into the auditorium for a college lecture, and you can turn to your right and left and see your peers as you would in the classroom. You can talk to them—even pass notes with them.

We aren't there yet, but this app will make you question how real the possibility will be. It makes you wish your were a kid—to learn about art by virtually visiting museums or learn about the moon by walking on it! The Vision Pro will make you excited for the future and it's apps like Keynote that help you see it.

FILES

If you download things from the Internet (or mail attachments) you'll be able to find them here. You'll also have access to all your cloud documents. Unfortunately, it's not terrible easy to search.

FACETIME AND PERSONAS

If you look around the Vision Pro OS, one thing you will notice quickly is there's no Facetime app. It's a strange thing, because the app does exists—you just won't find an icon for it. There's also no Phone icon—again, it exists, but there's no shortcut for them.

Instead, to make voice or Facetime calls, you'll go to the People area of the Home menu, then find the person you want to call, then on their contact card, you'll see Facetine as an option.

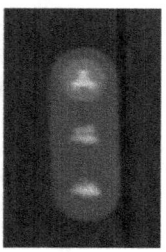

I say all this as a lead-in to Personas; there's no Personas app, but to take advantage of Facetime video calls, you'll need one.

Personas, as of this writing, is in beta. Don't let the beta label fool you, however, because it actually works really well—kind of. If you haven't tried the Vision Pro yet, then you've probably seen the memes of Personas or perhaps heard someone comment on how weird it looks. Chances are, you heard this from someone who hasn't used it on the Vision Pro and has only seen a photo. It's really something you need to experience with the headset on to fully appreciate.

My wife laughed when I called her; she laughed for a little too long! I suppose I could have did my hair. I'm also wearing a pink sweater in my photo, but for some reason it matches my skin and at first glance, makes it look like I'm not wearing a shirt!

Here's one of the biggest things you need to know about Personas: be careful what you wear! If you have a shirt collar that's crooked, that's what people will see until you redo your Persona. Personas is all about your face; that means your hair and clothing will appear stiff.

Make sure you have good lighting when you take your picture for Personas. If you have a webcam light, use it.

Creating a Persona is pretty quick, so experiment and have fun with it. Take a couple of pictures and see which one you like best.

Environments also change how things sound. If your environment is outdoors, you'll notice a very subtle change in how you sound to others. A lot of very fine details went into this experience, and this is one of them.

To anyone you call on the phone, you'll probably look a little—robotic. If you want to see why Personas is better than a meme, then try and find someone else with a Vision Pro to call—that's what Personas was really made for.

SETTING UP OR EDITING A PERSONA

If you didn't do a Persona at setup or you want to redo it, then you'll need to go into your settings to do it. Settings > Personas. From here you can either edit your Persona, or Recapture it.

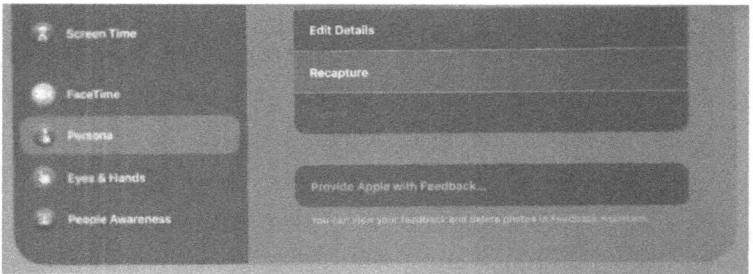

When you edit a Persona (or when you do it for the first time) you are able to pick the lighting of your Persona.

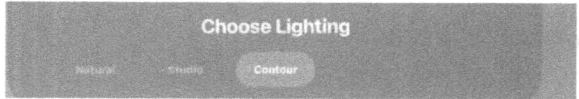

You can also pick the brightness and temperature of your skin tone.

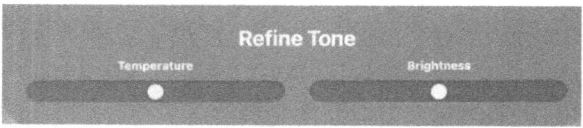

Finally, you can pick if you have glasses.

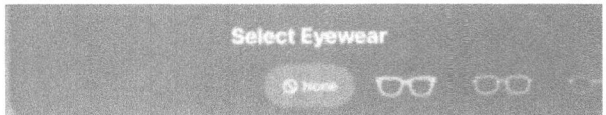

APP STORE

The App Store is not too different that the iPad app store. Here's the biggest thing to know: when you search for an app, it will automatically show you natively built apps; when the results come in, you can tap the compatible apps to see all apps. So if you are looking for something like Slack or Outlook (both are not currently available natively on Vision Pro) you would need to toggle over to compatible apps to find it.

To buy an app, you can use your password, or enable Optic ID—which means to buy something, you just stare at the screen and it confirms your identity with an eye scan.

COMPATIBLE APPS

Apps that are compatible with Vision Pro, but not built for Vision Pro (i.e. iPad apps) will show up in this section—that includes both Apple Apps and Apps you download from the App Store.

[5]

Taking and Viewing Pictures and Videos

TAKING SPACIAL VIDEOS AND PHOTOS WITH VISION PRO

Taking videos with your Vision Pro isn't bad, but, in my opinion, it's not as good as what you'll get on the iPhone 15 Pro. Vision Pro is better at viewing content than capturing it. But if you don't have an iPhone 15 Pro, then, for now, the Vision Pro is your only option—but don't be surprised if you start seeing Spacial capture appear on iPad and even the cheaper iPhone's in the future.

Capturing photos and videos is simple; there's no Camera app to open like you would on any other device. All you do is press down once on the top button.

Once you press down on the top button, it will ask if you want to capture a spacial photo or video.

Press the top button again to take the photo or video; if you are recording a video, you can can either press the top button to stop it, or press the red stop square.

You'll be able to share these photos and videos with anyone—even people without a Vision Pro. But to everyone else, they will appear in 2D.

TAKING SPACIAL VIDEOS AND PHOTOS WITH IPHONE 15 PRO

If you have an iPhone 15 Pro, then you may have already been capturing memories enhanced for the Vision Pro and not even known it! If you haven't then section will show you how (sorry, but this is only for the iPhone 15 Pro and Pro Max—regular iPhone 15 won't do it...nor will iPhone Pro's earlier than the 15).

SETTING UP YOUR IPHONE 15 PRO FOR SPATIAL VIDEO MAGIC

First things first, let's get your iPhone 15 Pro or Pro Max ready for this 3D journey. Head over to `Settings > Camera > Formats` and switch on the "Spatial video for Apple Vision Pro" option. This setting is your golden ticket to the 3D world, and is available for iPhone 15 Pro models running iOS 17.2 or later (it wasn't available when the phones first came out, so make sure and do that update if you haven't already).

RECORDING YOUR FIRST SPATIAL VIDEO

Ready to roll? Grab your iPhone 15 Pro, and let's get filming:

1. **Launch the Camera App**: Open up Camera and switch to Video mode. Landscape orientation is your friend here—portrait orientation isn't an option.
2. **Activate Spatial Video**: Look for the Spatial Video Off button and give it a tap. Now you're set to record in 3D!
3. **Capture the Moment:** Press the Record button or hit either volume button to start. Here are some pro tips for that perfect shot:
    a. Keep your iPhone stable and level.
    b. Position your subjects about 3 to 8 feet away.
    c. Ensure your lighting is bright and even.
4. **Wrap it Up**: Tap the Record button again or press a volume button to stop. To exit spatial video mode, just tap the Spatial Video On button.

VIEWING AND SHARING YOUR 3D CREATIONS

Make sure you're logged in with your Apple ID and have iCloud Photos on for seamless syncing across devices.

A QUICK NOTE ON SPECS

Remember, spatial videos on the iPhone 15 Pro and Pro Max are shot in 1080p at 30 fps. Each minute of this 3D goodness takes up about 130 MB of space, so plan your storage accordingly. That choir recital might end up taking over 4GB on your phone!

VIEWING PHOTOS

The Photos app is optimized for Vision Pro, but in a way, it's also an inferior app to what you get on iPhone and iPad; the Photos app is for viewing photos—not for editing them. It's organized in a very familiar way, but also feels like a reminder that the Vision Pro is a device to see content—not always edit content.

There's three main areas of the app. One the right is the main viewing area where all the thumbnails appear; next to that is the submenu that's based on what ever menu you select.

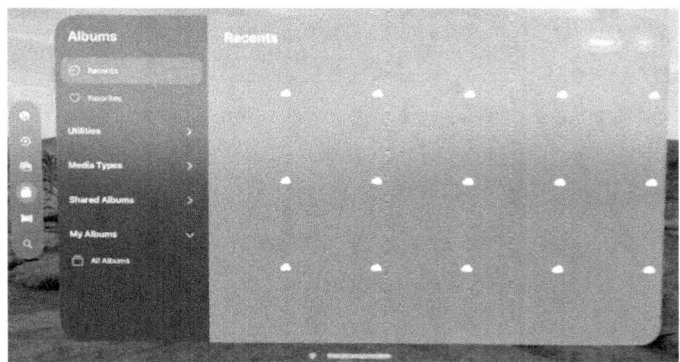

Finally, over on your right is the main menu, which shows: Spacial (where any spacial view shot on your iPhone or on the Vision Pro will show up, Memories (which you can create or Apple will create for you), Library (all photos), Albums, Panoramas, and Search.

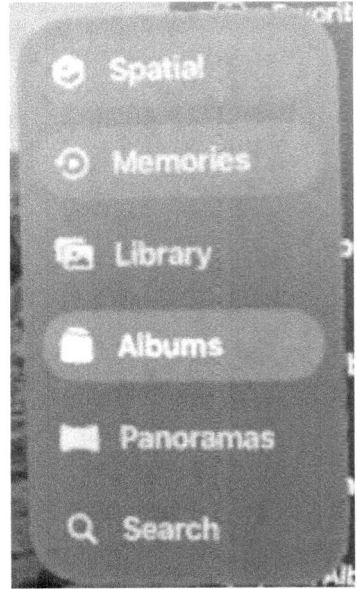

If you haven't tried the Search in a while, it's worth checking out. Don't think of it like searching for the titles of files; that's so yesterday! Search today lets you search for what's in the photos. So you can say "white dog" and it's able to understand what you just said and scan your photos for anything that resembles a white dog.

When you view your photo, you can share it and see it, but that's about it. Pinching and swiping will let you see the photos to the left and right, but, again, at this time there is not an option to edit a photo.

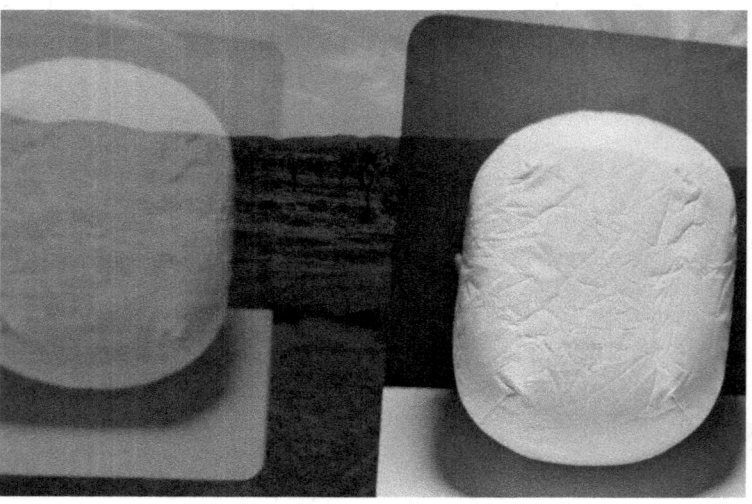

Next to Spacial videos (which, if you don't have a iPhone 15 Pro, it will probably be empty), the best thing about the app is Panoramas; and the great thing about Panoramas is you can take it with any phone—so you might have a few in your library.

When you view a Panorama on the Vision Pro, it will look like just a long photo. But take a look at that icon in the upper right corner—looks like a rectangle box that's being squeezed.

That turns your photo into an immersive 180 degree photo; you can't see it below, but in the headset, I'd be able to turn left and right to view the photo in very crisp HD.

Viewing Spacial photos and videos is a similar process; the normal view is 3D, but not immersive;

pressing on that corner icon will turn your Spacial photos and videos into an immersive experience. But be warned! Spacial videos can cause motion sickness! If you are watching this type of content, make sure there's not a lot of movement in the scene. I filmed my dogs playing and nearly fell over when I turned on the immersive mode!

[6]
SETTINGS

Now that you know your way around the Vision Pro, we're going to take a look at the settings, where you can see how to configure things.

The Settings app looks almost identical to the iPad; a left panel navigation with the settings for each category on the right. But don't let looks deceive you, because there's a lot of settings that you'll only find on Vision OS. I'll go over each area next.

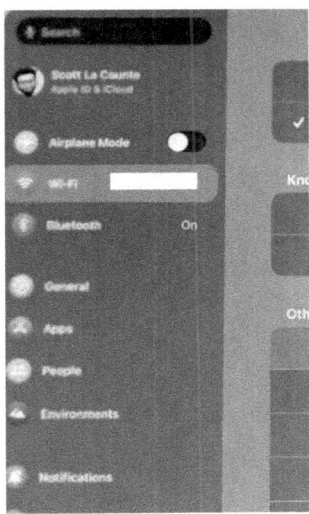

WI-FI

Anytime you want to change the wireless network that your Vision Pro is on, then you'll go here. It remembers passwords, so if you go into a location you've been before, it will automatically connect if the wi-fi is the same.

BLUETOOTH

What if you want to use a controller? Keyboard? Trackpad? Or another supported Bluetooth device? You do that in Bluetooth. Most controllers and keyboards are supported, but your best bet for a trackpad is the Apple one. When you use a trackpad, a small transparent circle will appear on your screen.

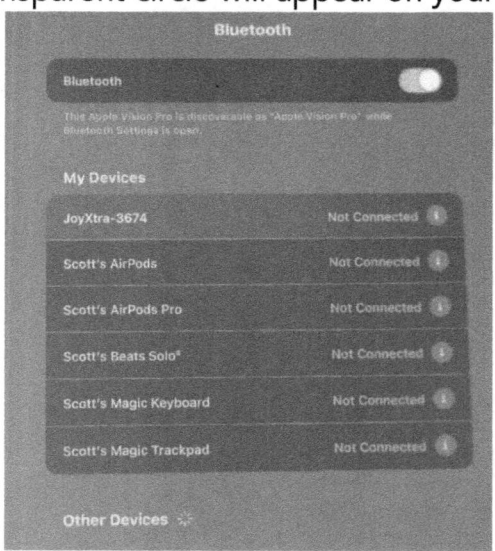

GENERAL

Some of the most important settings are found in General. Under about, you can get your devices serial number; you can also do software updates, change the keyboard look, adjust the time, change the language, add a VPN, reset your Vision Pro, and also shut it down.

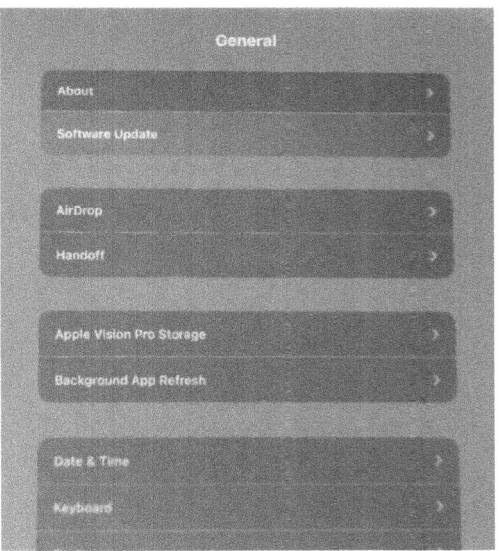

APPS

As the name implies, Apps is where you'll find a list of all your apps, but it's also where you go to change your app settings. When you tap on any app, you'll see additional things you can add or change.

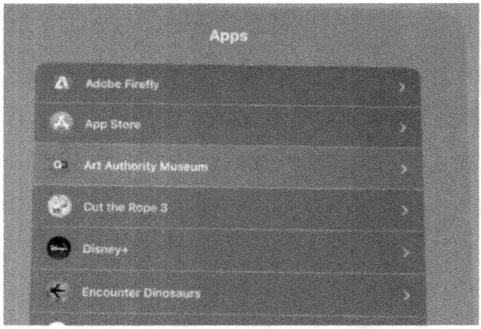

PEOPLE

People lets you adjust how names appear; it also lets you add people to your blocked list, so they can't contact you.

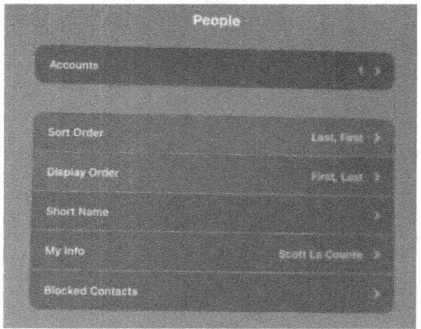

ENVIRONMENTS

Environments lets you pick if an environment is light, dark, or automatically changed based on here you are. The volume both below isn't for normal sound; it's for the ambient sound that plays in the environment—so if you're out the beach, you'll hear waves in the background, but you can adjust how loud they are.

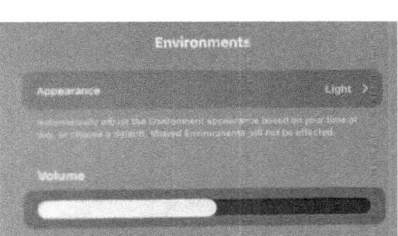

NOTIFICATIONS

Notifications lets you adjust the types of notifications you get from apps. So lets say you download the NBA app, but don't want notifications from them; you can toggle them off or, if you want them on, select how they appear.

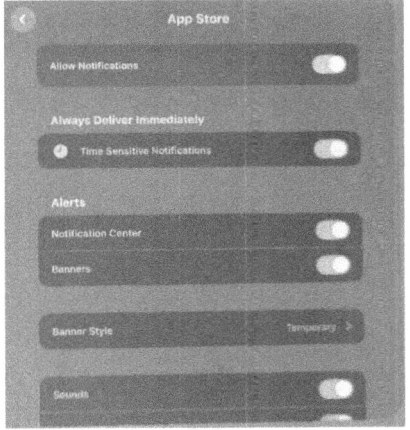

SOUNDS

Sounds lets you adjust the sound playing on your device.

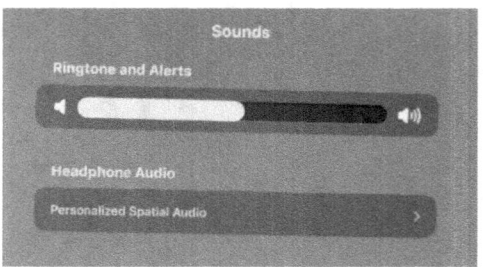

FOCUS

Focus lets you change what alerts appear; for example, you can set a mode where you won't get email or text notifications, but you still get phone calls from family members; or you can silence everything.

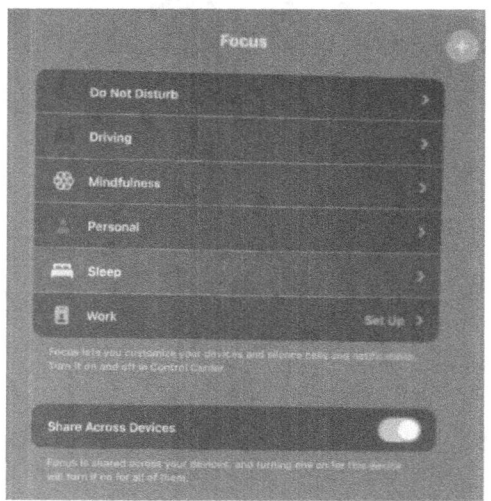

SCREEN TIME

If you got a Vision Pro, you probably love to consume entertainment, and you'll skip right over this one! But basically what it's for is to set different re-strictions—so you can only play games a certain number of hours or you can only watch PG-13 movies.

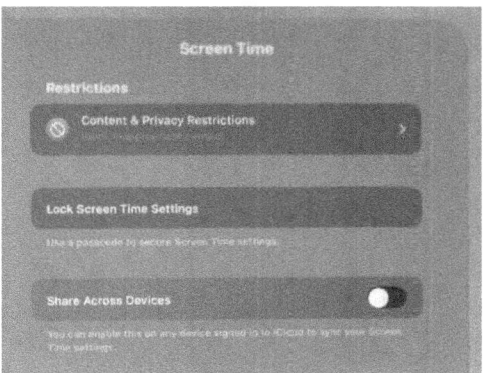

FACETIME

FaceTime is pretty basic in terms of settings; you can turn Siri and search on and turn FaceTime on and off; one thing you might want to do is add different emails and phone numbers, which is done in the bottom boxes (not shown in the illustration below).

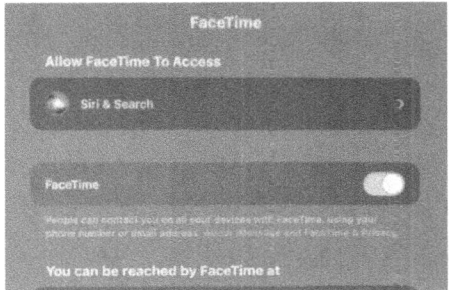

PERSONA

Persona is where you can make edits or recapture your Persona; it was covered in an earlier chapter.

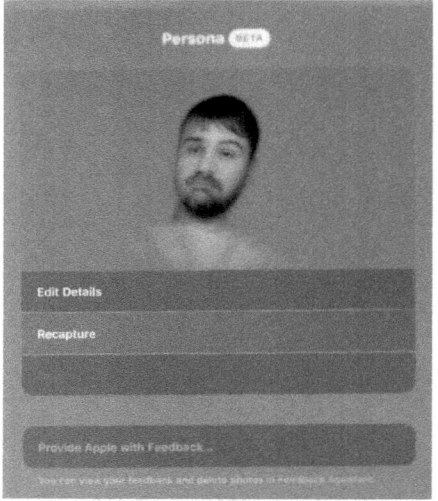

EYES & HAND

If hand and eye tracking don't seem to work, the first thing you should try is cleaning your lenes with the fabric that Apple included with your Vision Pro. You can also adjust the light. If that doesn't work, then you can go into this setting and redo the tracking. You might also want to try restarting your device. The tracking on the Vision Pro is incredible, but sometimes it does get a little...buggy—like you can't select corners or smaller buttons.

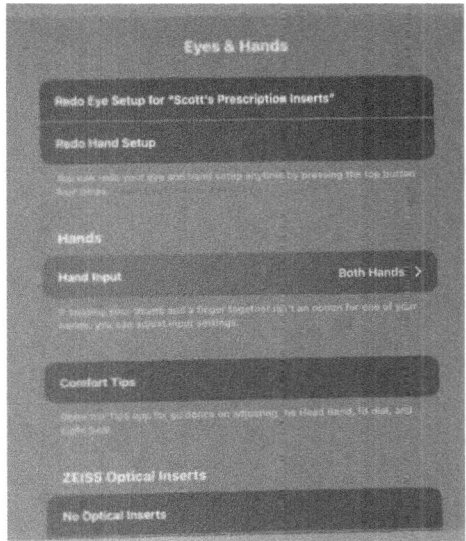

PEOPLE AWARENESS

When people walk up to you while you're wearing the headset, your environment will disappear, and you can see them. I think it's pretty cool and helps me not completely disappear from the world; but if you'd rather not see anyone, then you can toggle off people awareness in this setting. You can also pick if you want to see people when you are watching something immersive or only if you have up an environment.

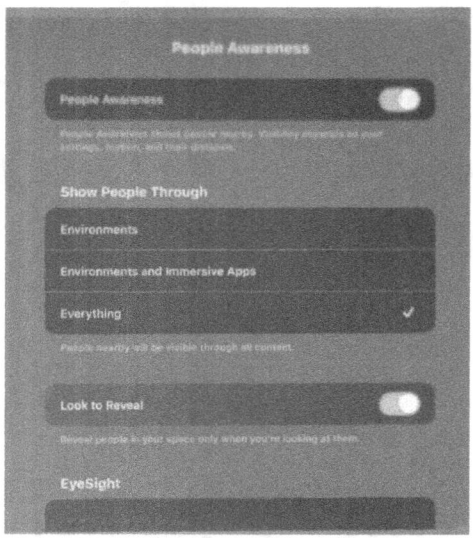

ACCESSIBILITY

Next to the General setting, Accessibility is the most comprehensive. You can go in here to reduce motion, add a hearing aide, make text bigger, and more much more.

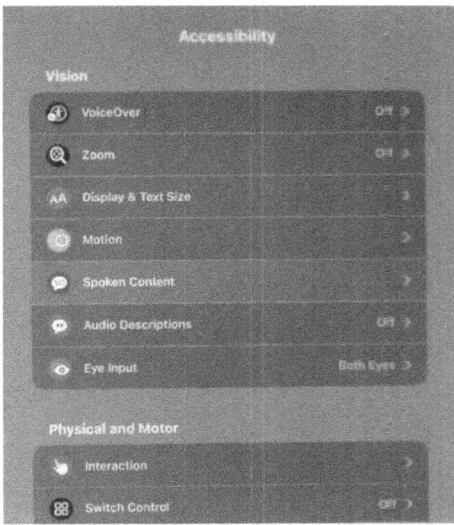

CONTROL CENTER

If you've never customized your support center, you should consider it. When you go into the Control Center settings, you can add and remove shortcuts that appear but pressing the + or – icon next to the shortcut. In VisionOS, you can also adjust the position of where it appears; if you want the icon to appear higher or lower, you can move the slider to find the best position.

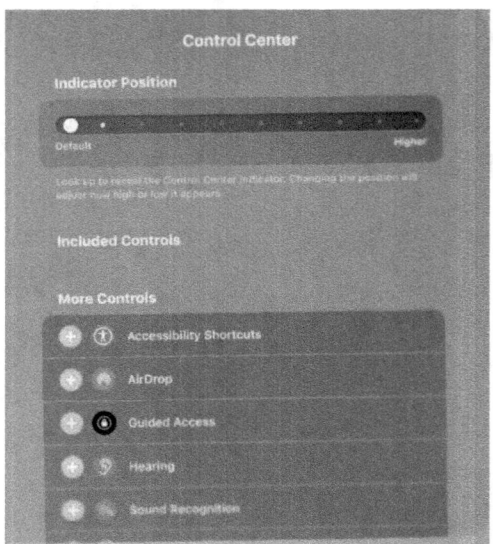

SIRI & SEARCH

If you want to change how Siri is activated, what the voice sounds like, and more, you can do so in this setting.

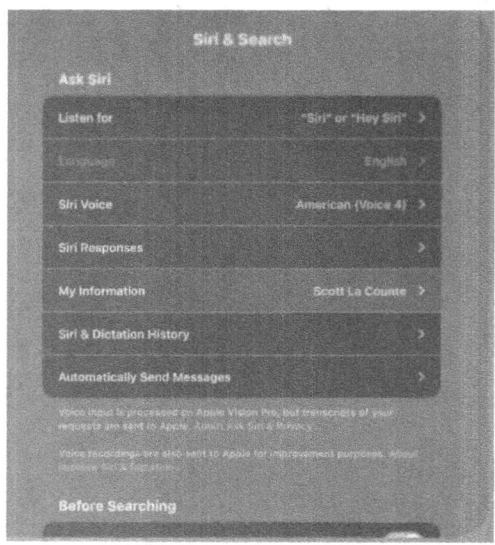

PRIVACY & SECURITY

Your apps track different things; it may track your location, for example; you can toggle that on and off here. But be careful—turning off tracking might change the behavior of the app; a weather app, for example, needs to know where you are to show you the weather of your location.

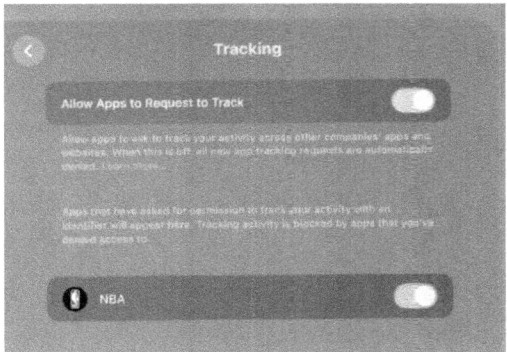

DISPLAY

If things appear to large or small, or to bright or dim, then you can go in here to adjust it.

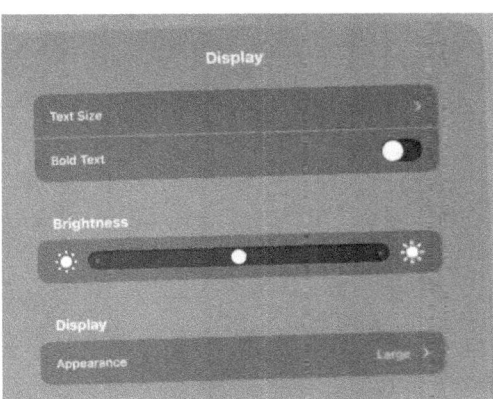

BATTERY

The battery section is very basic, as of this writing; it is just a toggle that lets you turn on and off the battery percent.

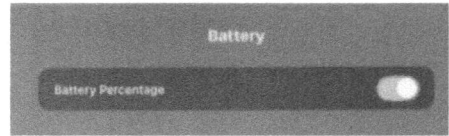

STORAGE

Storage will visualize where all your space is being used. Some things you can't do a lot about; for example, visionOS and System Data can't be reduced. Other things can either be offloaded or deleted to save on space.

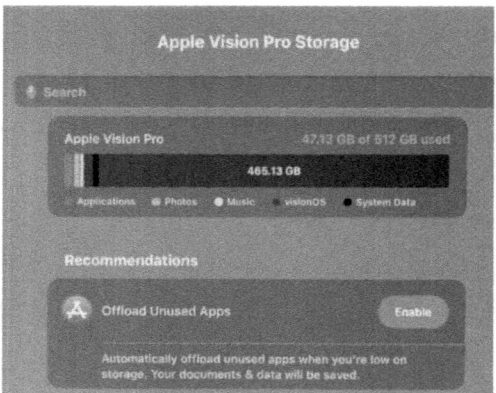

Scrolling down, you can see the amount of space each app in particular uses; some apps take several GB.

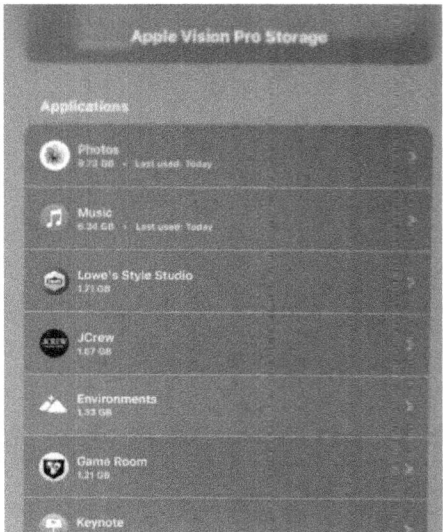

OPTIC ID & PASSCODE

Paying for things and using your password is a little different on Vision Pro; unlike other devices where you might use your fingerprint or face, Vision Pro uses your eyes. If you'd prefer to do somethings the old fashion way by typing in your password, you can toggle where it is used here.

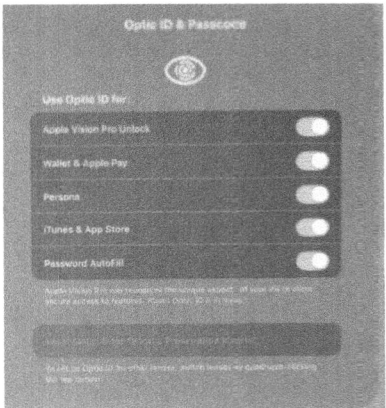

PASSWORDS

In the password section, you'll see both recommendations and what passwords were used; so if you can't remember what password you used for a specific website, you can go in here and see it.

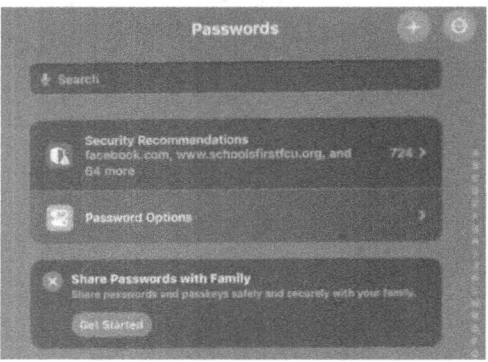

GAME CENTER

Game Center is what is used if you want to play games against friends or other users; it also lets you track game achievements. This section lets you turn it on, see your user name, and invite others to see you.

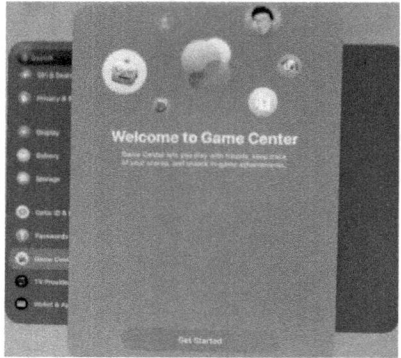

TV PROVIDER

If you subscribe to cable for TV, you can login to your provider in this section; this lets you watch certain apps without a subscription.

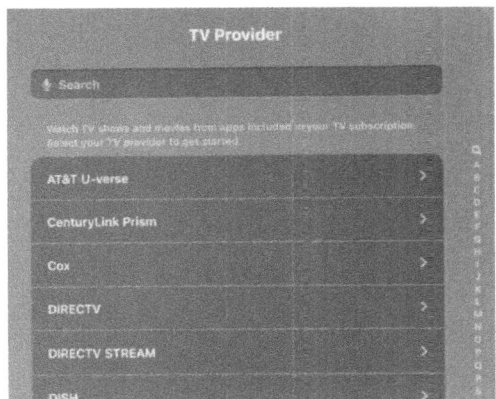

WALLET & APPLE PAY

Wallet is where all your payments are stored, and where you would go if you wanted to add a new credit card; you can also turn on and off Apple Cash here.

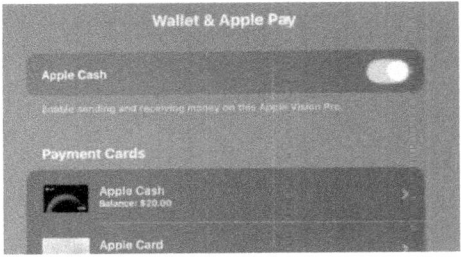

APPENDIX A: PROTECTING THE VISION PRO

Let's talk about keeping your cool new Vision Pro safe and sound. You've probably heard of AppleCare+, and for the Vision Pro, it's an option you might want to seriously consider. Here's the lowdown on what it offers and why it might just be a lifesaver for your device.

THE VISION PRO WARRANTY

Right off the bat, your Apple Vision Pro comes with a one-year hardware warranty and up to 90 days of complimentary tech support. That's pretty neat, but if you're looking for more comprehensive coverage, AppleCare+ is where it's at.

APPLECARE+

You can opt for a two-year coverage at $499 or go for a monthly plan at $24.99, which continues until you decide to cancel it.

Here's what you get with AppleCare+:

- **Accidental Damage Coverage**: We've all been there - accidents happen. With AppleCare+, you get unlimited incidents of accidental damage protection, though each incident carries a service fee. Think of it as a safety net for those oops moments.
- **Express Replacement Service**: Nobody likes being without their tech. With this service, you get a replacement device shipped to you, so you're not left in the lurch while yours is being fixed.
- **24/7 Expert Access**: Got a question at 2 AM? No problem. AppleCare+ gives you round-the-clock access to Apple experts.
- **Comprehensive Hardware Coverage**: This includes your Vision Pro, the battery, and even the included cable.

WHY CONSIDER APPLECARE+?

I'm sure you've felt a little...scammed...by a warranty. Is AppleCare+ a scam? Definitely not. It's peace of mind. Hopefully you'll never need it, but without it a simple cracked cover glass could set you back about $799, and other repairs might go as high as $2,399. Yikes! With AppleCare+, these costs are significantly reduced. For instance, other accidental damage is covered for $299 per incident.

GETTING APPLECARE+

How exactly do you get AppleCare+? There's two ways:

- **Buy When You Purchase**: The easiest way is to grab it when you're buying your Vision Pro.
- **60-Day Window**: Missed it at checkout? No worries. You've got 60 days from your device purchase to get AppleCare+ through the settings menu or at an Apple Store.

AppleCare+ for your Vision Pro is like having a trusty sidekick, ready to swoop in when things go sideways. So, whether you opt for the two-year deal or go monthly, it's an investment in peace of mind.

APPENDIX B: ACCESSORIES

The Vision Pro isn't Apple's most expensive device ever; that honor goes to the original Gold Apple Watches—remember those? Not many people do! But they maxed out at $17,000. Still, after spending over $3,500 on the headset, there's even more you'll have to consider buying from Apple (not including the $499 for Apple Care+).

I'm not including the ZEISS Optical Inserts here, because I wouldn't really call these optional accessories—if you wear prescription glasses, you'll need them.

APPLE VISION PRO TRAVEL CASE

The first thing you'll want to consider is a case. There will be plenty of third-party companies who make cases (Spigen was one of the first; they have a pretty nice one for just under $100) for the Vision Pro over the next few months and years, but if you want the official one from Apple, it will cost you $199.

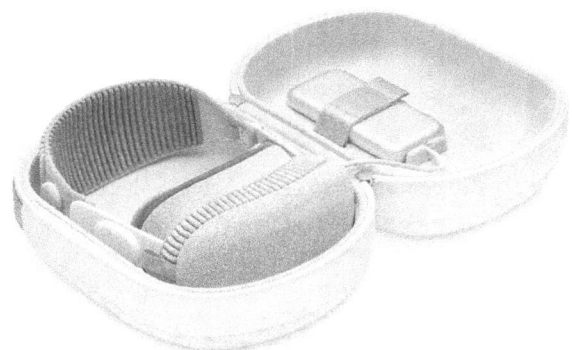

They call it a "travel case" but realistically, you'll probably want this for everyday use. It's a pretty durable headset, but most people will probably not feel comfortable tossing it on their couch or desk and walking away.

BELKIN BATTERY HOLDER FOR APPLE VISION PRO

There is currently only one third party company (aside from ZEISS) that Apple has partnered with on accessories: Belkin. The Vision Pro battery pack is something that is conveniently missing from a lot of the Vision Pro photos; it's not that Apple is hiding the fact that you need one–they probably just know it looks a lot more interesting when you don't have something dangling from the side of you. You can obviously put it in your pocket, or set it next to you, but for $49, Belkin has created a holder for the Battery pack, so you can also clip it to you.

Do you need it? It really depends on how you will use the Vision Pro. If you are sitting at your desk with it, the cord is long enough to set it down with no trouble at all; the same is true if you are watching a movie. Where things can get a little dicey is if you are doing a workout or moving around—especially if you are wearing something that doesn't have pockets. If you don't want to spend $49, this is one thing you'll probably find a lot of very cheap solutions for by other third party companies.

APPLE VISION PRO BATTERY

You can buy extras of almost every single part on the Vision Pro. Do you need to? If you are shar-ing the device with family members, and their head

size is bigger, then that might be a good investment. But for most people, the answer is no. One
thing, however, some people might want to pick
up is an extra battery for $199.

The Vision Pro will last about 2 hours in normal
use. If you're on a flight, that's probably not
enough time. But, and this is an important but, you
can charge the battery pack while you are using it.
You could also charge the battery pack with a USB-
C battery pack while you are using it. An extra battery pack might be more convenient for some people, but there's plenty of ways to keep using your
Vision Pro without it.

MAGIC KEYBOARD

The Vision Pro has a built-in on-screen keyboard. It also has very easy to use dictation. The keyboard takes a little getting used to, but it's pretty intuitive once you get the hang of it. Still, if you plan on using your Vision Pro alongside your Mac to get work done, a keyboard will be a nice to have. Apple's official solution is the Magic Keyboard for $99. You can technically use most bluetooth keyboards, however.

You also can pair the Vision Pro with trackpads and mouses. Should you? Again, it really comes down to comfort and how you use the Vision Pro. If your heavy on productivity and graphic design, then perhaps. Apple's official trackpad is $129, but you can use pretty much any bluetooth mouse you may have at your desk. That said, eye tracking is far superior to on-screen typing, so you might want to try it out before you spend the extra money on a mouse.

Personally, I have an Apple mouse and keyboard, and I picked up a fitted acrylic tray (it was about $30 on Amazon) to put them in; so when I'm using my Vision Pro for work, I have the keyboard and mouse in my lap (see below image).

AIRPODS PRO (2ND GENERATION)

The Vision Pro's sound will probably blow you away—and also annoy the person sitting next to you, who can't see what you see! If you are around others and need sound, then the AirPods Pro is a good investment (2nd generation also has USB-C charging). You can technically use any bluetooth headset, but only the AirPods Pro has spacial audio.

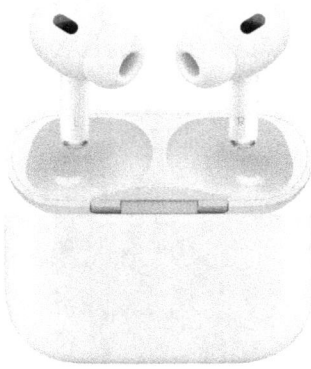

SONY PLAYSTATION® DUALSENSE™ WIRELESS CONTROLLER

The last thing you may want to pick up is a game controller. Apple is promoting the Sony controller ($69.95) on the Apple Store app, but most gaming controllers will work just fine.

Anything on the Vision Pro will work without a controller, but some games will work better if you have one.

INDEX

ABOUT THE AUTHOR

Scott La Counte is a UX Designer and writer. His first book, *Quiet, Please: Dispatches from a Public Librarian* (Da Capo 2008) was the editor's choice for the Chicago Tribune and a Discovery title for the Los Angeles Times.

He has written dozens of best-selling how-to guides on tech products.

He teaches UX Design for U.C. Berkeley.

You can connect with him at ScottDouglas.org.

www.ingramcontent.com/pod-product-compliance
Lightning Source LLC
Chambersburg PA
CBHW071044290526
45795CB00004B/1313